KIKI

McDONOUGH

A LIFE OF COLOUR

KIKI

McDONOUGH

A LIFE OF COLOUR

40 Years of Gemstone Jewellery

Text by ISABELLE SPURWAY

Foreword by CAROL WOOLTON

First published in Great Britain in 2025 by Papadakis Publisher
An imprint of Academy Editions Limited

⯈P PAPADAKIS

Kimber Studio, Winterbourne, Berkshire, RG20 8AN, UK
info@papadakis.net | www.papadakis.net

🅕 🅞 🅛 @papadakisbooks

Publishing Director: Alexandra Papadakis
Design Director: Aldo Sampieri
Editor: Molly Dewar
Publishing Assistant: Abi Evans

Front cover: A pair of fire opal and diamond earrings from the 2025 Fireworks collection
Back cover: A fire opal and diamond necklace designed to celebrate 40 years of Kiki McDonough
Frontis: A selection of gemstone bracelets set in 18ct gold

ISBN 978 1 906506 76 6

Printed and bound in China

A CIP catalogue of this book is available from the British Library

MIX
Paper | Supporting
responsible forestry
FSC
www.fsc.org   FSC® C008047

Papadakis is committed to a sustainable future for our business, our readers, and our planet. This book is made from Forest Stewardship Council™ certified paper, responsibly sourced from forests that are managed in an environmentally and socially responsible manner.

ACKNOWLEDGMENTS

To my mother, who was so chic and beautiful. She imbued me with my work ethic, and always said it was tiresome to complain.

To my father, who sadly died before he could see the fruits of my labour, but being a jeweller himself I think he would have been proud of what I have achieved, albeit rather surprised.

I would like to thank Nigel Milne for starting me off on the road to fine jewellery. He changed my life, and I am so grateful.

I wish to thank all the people who have worked for me over the past 40 years who have helped me build the Kiki brand. I couldn't have done this without them and I am so grateful for their support, inspiration, and enthusiasm. So many of them keep in touch and I have loved watching them develop their lives.

David Deakin and Stephen Brady, who worked with me for the first 20 years, and helped me navigate the world of jewellery and design.

Isabelle Spurway, who has helped me write this book, and listened to all my endless stories with patience and a ready smile.

David McDonough and Randle Siddeley, my two ex-husbands who continue to be so supportive and remain great friends.

My Managing Director, Sian Daley, who has worked so hard to make me more familiar with the workings of corporate life. I am not sure what she thought she was getting into when she first arrived, but, luckily for me, she is still here.

Finally, and most importantly, all my lovely clients who have bought my jewellery over the years and have kept me going with their love of the coloured gemstones which are my passion. I am so grateful to them all.

An amethyst, peridot, green amethyst, and diamond neckalce set in 18ct gold

CONTENTS

PREFACE

This book is about a girl who thought school was annoying, trained as a secretary, and eventually built a worldwide brand on her own.

It has been the most wonderful, joyous experience, with more challenges than I ever could have imagined back in 1985, but I wouldn't change it for the world.

This book is dedicated to my two sons William and Edward who have never complained about having a working mother and have always supported me with humour and enthusiasm. I am so proud of them.

*A pair of fire opal, peridot, and diamond earrings set in 18ct
yellow gold from the 2023 Special Editions collection*

FOREWORD

by Carol Woolton

The eternal challenge for a designer is to make pieces which are relevant and modern as well as timeless. Creating objects with the intention of imbuing them with a sense of beauty and significance is an art form, but when the object in question is jewellery, there's the added complication of wearability. No easy task. When these various disciplines align in a successful outcome it's quite an accomplishment. The fact that Kiki McDonough has achieved this in countless collections over forty years is nothing short of a triumph.

The jewellery carries artistic elements and values from Kiki herself, reinvigorated every season by the changing narratives she observes, fuelled by her eye for shape and colour from the natural world. Yes, she does use white diamonds - indeed her Kiki Tiara blazing with starburst rays of diamonds was exhibited at Sotheby's Auction House, but for the legions of loyal fans and glossy magazines who feature her – Kiki means colour.

Even from the beginning of her career when the overarching trend in jewels was white, Kiki introduced London to fascinating colours in pastel gemstones that the majority of people hadn't seen before. Trays of mouth-watering soft green beryls, amethysts, yellow citrine, aquamarines, peridots, and pink morganite invariably twinkle in her windows. She has a singular eye for unusual cuts and the unorthodox beauty of bright or pale blush-coloured stones that she sources worldwide. What's the secret to her success? There's a lot of hard work, focus, and attention to detail, but it may chiefly be because she makes it easy for women to look good. Her jewellery flatters and brings joy.

From the early days in the West End to Walton Street and now housed in Symons Street people are drawn to her stores. Sometimes they just happen to be passing by and are struck by a sparkle in the window, other times it might be a member of the Royal Family, a celebrity, a regular client or perhaps one of their daughters, because if you can master timeless, new generations will always discover you. In this changing world her vision is well placed to survive fast-paced changes in fashion. The landscape in London has altered beyond recognition over the years as the big brands arrived to dominate the city, which makes Kiki's achievement all the more remarkable. Quite simply, she's a stalwart of the British jewellery industry. Her special talent, style, and success are being ever more widely recognised and I, like many others, hope there will always be a corner by Sloane Square that provides beautiful life-enhancing British jewellery.

INTRODUCTION

Kiki McDonough, the colourful, enduring, fine jewellery brand was founded in 1985 by Kiki McDonough after she fell into jewellery design and decided to run with it. Over forty years, Kiki has built a much-loved, globally renowned brand, designing a multitude of sought-after and timeless pieces. It is no surprise that The Queen and The Princess of Wales often turn to their Kiki pieces when dressing for royal occasions. One of the first women to make a name for herself in the luxury jewellery world, Kiki has built a well-respected business on her own, whilst also juggling two sons, multiple patronages, and a social life that would tire most twenty-somethings.

Kiki in her Chelsea-based office

Kiki's brand started as a concession in a friend's antique jewellery shop in 1985 when he asked her if she would design some modern jewellery, the result of which (a pair of heart crystal earrings with a diamond bow on top) are now in the modern jewellery collection of the Victoria & Albert Museum, London. Kiki has designed jewellery ever since, and the brand has grown significantly over the past forty years. Now much admired and with a rightful place on the global luxury stage, Kiki McDonough is known for creating vibrant, colourful, fine jewellery that can be worn every day. Having been in the business for four decades, Kiki has seen buying patterns change over the years, and has witnessed first-hand the transition from men buying gifts for their partners to women buying the jewellery they want for themselves. One of the first jewellers to popularise coloured gemstones outside of the big three (rubies, emeralds, and sapphires), Kiki creates jewellery with a multitude of beautiful colours which speak to the stylish modern woman. The ethos of the brand is that jewellery should be worn every day, rather than sit collecting dust in a jewellery box, so her designs can take you from the office to a fancy restaurant, and everywhere in between.

Kiki is a fifth-generation jeweller, and the first woman in that line, however the journey of building a brand has not always been smooth sailing. She has steered her business through myriad challenges: two recessions, a pandemic, political instability, and the chaos that comes with raising a family. To look back and reflect on the journey of the brand is to look back and reflect on the trajectory of her life, and reaching any anniversary is both nostalgic and contemplative. "*It has been a fascinating journey*", Kiki reflects, "*and one which I feel very privileged to have had*". Even now, Kiki remains energetic and enthusiastic about her business, always ready with a witty quip, preparing to rush out for a lunch and mentally noting what she needs to get done before her evening engagement. Even at seventy, she is not slowing down. Jewellery is as important now as it was forty years ago. It has remained, and will remain, the mark of an important occasion, a form of self-expression, a way to say *I love you* to someone, or to yourself. The legacy Kiki will leave is her desire to make these important moments more colourful, and it is a legacy that will continue to inspire the future of her business.

A pair of fire opal and diamond earrings set in 18ct yellow gold from the Kiki Diamonds collection

A young Kiki at a children's party

THE BEGINNING

*Kiki and her beloved brother Julian
whom she nicknamed 'Chebb'*

Those fortunate enough to have met Kiki will agree there is no doubt that she is a force with which to be reckoned. Tatler magazine once wrote, *"Kiki is the nicest woman in retail, but don't cross her!"* Charming and interesting, Kiki loves to recount tales of glamorous parties and exotic trips alongside the unpretentious chatter of her work and family life. She is a woman who has clearly lived fully, taken every opportunity offered to her with great enthusiasm, and reaped the benefits of one who sees life as an adventure rather than a chore. She knows what she wants, and she knows she will need to work hard to get it. In Kiki's living room there is a painting which captures her essence almost exactly; a portrait of her standing, one hand on her slender hip, looking contemplative with five strings of pearls around her neck and large citrine earrings beneath her short brown hair. Her second husband, the famous landscape designer Randle Siddeley (also known as Lord Kenilworth), commissioned Howard Morgan to paint this portrait but refused to take it in the end because Kiki's eyes weren't quite perfect, eyes which he rightly deemed her most telling and important feature. It wasn't until Kiki met Morgan at a party five years later and awkwardly apologised for the situation that she acquired the painting for herself. And with it, her position as a strong, self-sufficient woman went pride of place on her wall for her many guests to see. She has always been like this, it seems, independent and no-nonsense, wanting to sprint off into the world and make friends with as many people as possible. Her mother used to say that Kiki was born with a party invitation in her hand, and Kiki herself acknowledges that she never has been able to sit still. Once, when she was a child, her parents arranged for her to have a tea party with all her school friends at their house in Chelsea, and young Kiki quite literally could not contain her excitement. Her temperature rose, and a fever began, and the party had to be cancelled. It seems there is no person in the world better suited to life as a business-owner-socialite than Kiki.

*A teenage Kiki (centre) at her boarding school linking
arms with the other girls*

| House Report | Caroline still is far too noisy, and continues to break rules. Most of her faults spring from her happy nature, but she must try next turn to calm down. House Mistress D Duffy |
| General Report | Still inconsistent. We wish that Caroline would apply her excess energy to her work. M. Wilson. Form Mistress |

Kiki's school report from her boarding school:

*"Caroline still is far too noisy, and continues to break rules. Most of her faults spring from
her happy nature, but she must try next term to calm down."*

"Still inconsistent. We wish that Caroline would apply her excess energy to her work."

EARLY YEARS

Chelsea born and bred, Kiki reflects on her childhood in a house just off the King's Road fondly. She describes her young self as 'un-spoilt' yet blissfully happy. Her memories of childhood involve long, happy hours in the gardens at the Royal Hospital, Chelsea, making friends with other girls and crashing their family picnics ("*my new friend has invited me for lunch!*" Kiki would tell her mother when she came to collect her wayward child from another family). She would spend long afternoons sitting on the grass, picking forget-me-nots and making daisy chains, before the Sergeant Duke would blow his whistle to scare the children away from the flowers.

Some of Kiki's fondest memories include a ballet class she attended as a young girl, to which she would look forward all week, and indeed was the beginning of a lifelong love for ballet. She would always be the first in the studio, excited for her teacher, Miss Ballentyne, to start the class. Dancing well was extremely important to Kiki, because whoever danced the best in the class would be given an orange smartie. She still affectionately associates the chocolate with her childhood ballet lessons.

When Kiki was six, her brother, Julian, was born, and young Kiki was immediately besotted with him. A feisty child, and already very defensive of the people she loved, Kiki would always stand up for Julian during their childhood and would scold their mother whenever she berated him.

Kiki attended "*endless different schools*", because "*school bored [her]*", and spent much of her time looking out of the window, desperate to leave education behind and experience all the excitement and adventure the world had to offer. She credits a dreadful and gruelling stint at an all-girls boarding school in the 60s as the reason for her independence and capabilities. Originally excited about the adventure of boarding school, the unkind, snidey, all-girls environment was more unbearable than enjoyable. In addition to the unpleasant atmosphere, the girls were skinny and constantly hungry, allowed to bathe twice a week and disciplined quickly (sometimes for wearing coloured underwear). They did, however, have to think and make decisions for themselves, resulting in many strong, self-reliant women.

After leaving boarding school (it took the threat of running away for Kiki's parents to finally let her leave), Kiki finished her schooling at Queen's Gate, London, but the most important thing she learnt during this time was *"what size Biba boots [she] needed and how quickly [she] could get to the front of the queue"*. She made friends easily here, away from the intensity of an all-girls boarding school environment, and school became a form of social entertainment. Shopping, learning how to get out of a sports car without being too provocative, and curating documents with her friends like the NSIT list, which stated those boys who were 'not safe in taxis', filled up most of Kiki's time. With all this, there weren't many hours left in the day for such tedious things as maths and Latin. Kiki's teachers included the soon-to-be head of MI5, Eliza Manningham-Buller (whom Kiki says was *"rather scary"*), and booker prize winner Penelope Fitzgerald, but Kiki and her friends weren't to appreciate this at the time: they were all too busy having a good time.

KIKI'S PARENTS

Kiki remembers her father being extremely strict with her during her last year of school and afterwards, because at eighteen he had been in a prisoner of war camp, and at that same age Kiki was "*running around London, going to parties every night and coming home at two in the morning*". Kiki's father, Robin Axford, a fourth-generation jeweller of Harvey & Gore in Burlington Gardens off Bond Street, began his career in the family shop after the Second World War, when he returned from four years in Polish and German prisoner-of-war camps after being captured at Dunkirk. As soon as Robin returned from the war, his father made it clear there was to be no hanging around the house, and gave his son a month to get out and find work. After the harshness of his internment, some of which was in solitary confinement, one month appeared an unfair bargain. He did, however, eventually find stillness and contentment in jewellery, with which he found a total affinity. He became a world expert in Georgian jewellery and English silver, and people used to come from all over the world to show him pieces and seek his opinion. Even Queen Mary of Teck would visit the shop sometimes, and she was so terrifying everyone on the shop floor would hurry down to the basement leaving the poor porter to serve her alone. A man who took immense pleasure in learning the stories and meaning behind the pieces he was

Kiki's parents, Robin Axford and Yvonne Axford

shown, the post-war spike in breaking apart elaborate and expertly made jewellery for money affected Kiki's father a great deal. Customers would bring in the most remarkable pieces, Edwardian tiaras and intricately hand-crafted Georgian jewellery, and ask him to disassemble them to sell the parts. To many people, these pieces were relics that had better use as cash in those desperate times, but to Robin, they were taking apart vital historical artefacts. He was a gentle soul, most likely because he had seen so much brutality during the war, and he only wanted people to be kind. Kiki remembers her father as "*immensely knowledgeable*", but wasn't convinced by his skills as a businessman, though his love for jewellery and head-down approach to working has always influenced the way she views work and the industry. His advice to Kiki was "*never judge a book by its cover*", and "*nothing is cheap, just inexpensive*", two mantras by which Kiki has stuck in her own business. Robin also had a wonderful sense of humour, something he passed down to his daughter, and a love for writing poetry.

In the memorial edition of *Other Men's Flowers*, an anthology of poems collated by A. P. Wavell during the Second World War, a poem by an 'ordinary soldier', written in the wake of Wavell's death, closes the book. This poem, penned by Robin, is a heartfelt tribute to a man he had strongly admired. Though Robin was always very reserved and tight-lipped about his feelings,

A poem written by Robin Axford from the 1982 memorial edition of 'Other Men's Flowers' collated by the late Lord Wavell and printed by Butler and Tanner

poetry served as an emotional outlet throughout his life, and his words in *Other Men's Flowers* have resonated with and touched many people.

Kiki's mother, on the other hand, was a strong-willed and stylish woman. Yvonne Axford, (or Mrs A, as she was known to Kiki's employees) was French, and extremely pragmatic. She had worked at Galeries Lafayette in Paris and London organising fashion shows after the Second World War, and was always chic and elegantly put together, acutely aware of the fashion world and the prominent place it held in society. Unlike Robin, who viewed the jewellery in his shop as valuable historical objects, Mrs A knew the merit jewellery held as modern accessories. She would try to give him advice on the running of his business, but Robin wanted a quiet life, so little of it was ever implemented. Mrs A had a fire beneath her, and Kiki's get-up-and-go attitude certainly came from her mother.

One of Kiki's earliest memories of her mother involves a car ride down the A3 motorway, driving to Kiki's boarding school after half-term break:

Yvonne Axford (Mrs A) in Battersea

"*You must behave yourself this term*," said Mrs A. "*I am sick to death of driving up and down the A3 to see your house mistress.*"

To which Kiki replied, "*But she is horrible. I hate her and she hates me.*"

"*I know,*" said Mrs A, "*she is absolutely ghastly. But you must behave yourself because it's costing me a fortune in petrol.*"

No-nonsense and constantly on life's case, Mrs A was firm, but fair, and refused to bend to her daughter's complaining, or justify her bad behaviour. Her view that people should have simply gotten on with things whether they liked them or not was shared with many others who lived through the uncertainty and hardship of the Second World War, and was often passed on to their children. Like Robin, Mrs A knew the value of hard work and, to help the war effort and 'do her bit', learnt to drive, and travelled around Great Britain delivering books to soldiers at prisoner-of-war camps. By day, she was a strong, unconventional, working woman tackling the Welsh hills in a van filled with paperbacks, and by night she was dressed to the nines, perfectly put together. This combination of work and play is something Kiki learnt to implement in her own life, and she had a fantastic role model. Though Kiki's parents did end up separating – Kiki reflects her mother was far too tough to be with someone so gentle – Kiki credits her adaptable nature to the two sides inherited from each parent: her father's creativity and her mother's practicality.

REBELLIOUS TEENAGE YEARS & SERIAL JOBBING

A highly spirited and slightly rebellious teenager, Kiki's teenage years and early twenties were filled with parties, dances, and competitions with her friends to see who could go the longest without falling asleep. Forty-eight hours was Kiki's record. *"God, King's Road was so alive"*, she recalls, thinking back to her time frequenting pubs on the famous road, dressed in her bell bottoms and a floppy hat. Kiki and her friends would trail endlessly around the shops on King's Road or the stalls at Kensington Market on Saturdays, looking for new bell bottoms and badges to put on them, silver jewellery and Afghan coats. When she wasn't in Chelsea, she spent time at her friend's houses in the countryside, where there would be house parties most weekends. Rock 'n' Roll was all the rage, and dances were raucous affairs, places to smoke and drink and make new friends. After tiring themselves out with partying, they would sit around in each other's sitting rooms, listening to the distinctive, smooth voice of Bob Dylan, and putting the world to rights.

As soon as she was able to leave school behind, Kiki went straight into the working world as a secretary and began her career in the fashion room at Vogue. She remained there for a year and a half but became *"uncomfortable"* with the fact that *"everything was about clothes all day long"*, so soon left. She would take up numerous other positions over the next few years, including working for David Sterling, who founded the SAS, and a position as a secretary in Mrs Thatcher's letter-writing office, but nothing stuck for long. For Kiki, these jobs were dull and tedious, and for many years afterwards she kept a job advert from the 70s stuck to her desk as a motivator and reminder that she had to work hard, or else she would be organising somebody else's travel, writing their letters (shorthand required), and generally doing things that bored her. University was never on the cards, not only because women didn't tend to go to university in those days unless they were ridiculously intelligent, but also because Kiki had no interest in academia. If she had her time again, she would still choose to dive straight into work.

During this time of serial jobbing, Kiki married David McDonough, her first husband, when she was twenty-four. The two met when Kiki was nineteen at an Oxford University party, and their friendship only strengthened when Kiki took up a temporary position as a secretary for David. Kiki describes the two of them in a room working together as *"hilarious"*, both of them quick-witted and quick to laugh, and swiftly their friendship turned into romance. Her parents had always stressed the importance of finding a successful husband, preferably an accountant, and the expectation was that Kiki would take a job for a few years, get married, have children, and give up work altogether. This path was far too straightforward and boring for Kiki, and she had no desire to slow down when things were only starting to get exciting. Were her parents proud of her for starting her own business? *"I think my father thought it was a sweet little thing for me to do"*, Kiki says, though he died only six years after she set up Kiki McDonough, so he wouldn't see its long-term success. Women building and running businesses was still seen as an anomaly in the 80s, especially to older men who were so used to gender stereotypes, so, unsurprisingly, Robin didn't expect his daughter's brand to take flight. Mrs A, on the other hand, lived to see the business trade for thirty-eight years and worked for the company herself on and off until her nineties, first on the shop floor, and then behind the scenes as a pearl stringer. Though Mrs A never congratulated Kiki on a job well done (*"in those days you didn't get praise"*), Kiki knows that her mother was proud of her and everything she achieved over the years. When Mrs A passed away, Kiki found clippings of Kiki McDonough jewellery from magazines and newspaper articles about Kiki herself stashed away in her belongings, a quiet and loving way of expressing admiration.

A youthful Kiki and David on holiday in France

It wasn't always Kiki's dream to be a jeweller. Her favourite toy as a child was a miniature grocery shop, and Kiki remembers it so specifically: a weighing scale, a cash register, a few pieces of plastic fruit, a pork chop, and tiny brown paper bags. Her other favourite was a china tea set, and she took great joy in asking people for tea. She played with these toys constantly, and her love of people and selling must have grown and blossomed from these activities she loved so dearly as a child. What she could never have foreseen, back then, was how the many elements that had influenced her life would work together to make her an important name in the jewellery world. Her love of socialising and parties, her experience and comfort with fine jewellery, her dream to one day run a shop. Some would call it luck, which Kiki acknowledges played an important part, but to know Kiki is to know that this future was inevitable. If anyone could have told the young girl with the minuscule grocery shop what her life would one day look like, she would most likely have fainted from excitement.

16C GRAFTON STREET, LONDON W1X 3LF

TEL. 01 409 0255

A selection of haematite and rock crystal pieces from Kiki's 1980s collections

1980s

A haematite necklace with a central bow motif

HOW IT ALL STARTED

The beginning of Kiki's eponymous brand came as quite a surprise to her. Whilst she confessed she hadn't the slightest idea how to design jewellery for the modern day, and found the whole idea of doing so strange, her husband at the time, David McDonough, convinced her to give it a go. It saved her from a rather dull job, working in a warehouse for a leather accessories company, and Kiki has always been one to accept a challenge. Trained originally as a secretary, and a complete novice, Kiki arrived at her new position in Nigel Milne's shop on Grafton Street, Mayfair, with a sketchbook and pencil in hand, wondering how on earth she would make it work. With a family background in antique jewellery and a father with his own shop, Kiki grew up around all sorts of wonderful creations, and she credits this as one of the reasons she is so comfortable around fine jewellery. When she was a child, her father would bring home various pieces to show her, produce expensive brooches and necklaces from his pocket and slide them to Kiki down the table like a cowboy's beer at the bar, so handling expensive jewellery has never made her nervous.

A pair of rock crystal heart earrings and a haematite and rock crystal necklace,
both with gold and diamond bows, from Kiki's 1980s collections

Kiki's first collection included a large, 80s, heart-shaped crystal motif with gold bows and a single diamond, in earrings and pendants. Inspired by a vintage brooch in one of the antique cabinets in the shop with a round crystal, diamond-set flower and pearl surround, these pieces were modern enough to satisfy trend-chasing clientele with their heavy gold settings, yet classic enough to invest in. After designing these earrings, Kiki found a manufacturer named David Deakin who eyed her sketches with scepticism and told her, kindly, that he didn't think they would sell. Kiki laughed and agreed, but they got on so well they went forward with production anyway, and their working relationship would go on to last twenty-five years. To their surprise, the earrings were put on the shelf at Nigel Milne's, and people bought them. It was a pair of these very first earrings that would go on to be featured in the modern jewellery collection at the Victoria & Albert Museum as an example of pioneering modern jewellery. In the first four years of business, around five hundred of the crystal earrings sold, so it seemed Kiki and David had struck gold. Kiki wasn't to know it then, but this was the beginning of a long and successful career in jewellery design.

After this initial triumph, Kiki went to her father and asked for a £5,000 loan to set up her jewellery business, ("*he looked at me like I had just dropped out of planet Zog!*" exclaims Kiki) and he agreed, so long as she paid him back within two years, with interest. Kiki was rather pleased, and Robin rather surprised, when she paid him back only a year later. The country was under the lead of prime minister Margaret Thatcher at the time, and Kiki describes "*the most amazing can-do atmosphere*" which encouraged the entrepreneurial spirit of countless people. It was during this time that many women launched their own businesses, and Kiki was in good company, with famous handbag designer Anya Hindmarch and fashion designer Amanda Wakeley starting their own trailblazing brands nearby in London. To watch a woman become prime minister in a man's world was an inspiration for women across the country, and though Margaret Thatcher is remembered as a divisive figure in politics, the spirit she inspired has not, in Kiki's opinion, been repeated since.

I am thrilled to be able to launch my first collection under the same roof as my friend and business partner, Nigel Milne.

Our new venture is based on the firm belief that those people who enjoy wearing real jewellery, modern or antique, should be offered a wider choice of jewellery, with the old and the new sitting comfortably alongside each other.

With Nigel's guidance and encouragement, I have designed a range of what I hope you will think are both stylishly fashionable, highly wearable, and affordable pieces. I hope, too, that you will find their versatility appealing.

Above all, like my antique paste collection, my jewellery cries out to be worn with flair and panache. Do come and see me in the shop to try on some of the pieces and see for yourself.

I look forward to seeing you in Grafton Street.

Kiki McDonough

– Kiki McDonough

Kiki introducing her brand in the first Kiki McDonough catalogue

80s EXTRAVAGANCE & KIKI'S FIRST COLLECTION

The 80s were filled with fashion that was wackier and bolder than anything that had come before. Hair was set and styled so it sat at least five inches from a woman's head, and power suits with masculine frames were a promise from women that they were about to take over. "*We all looked like the Hunchback of Notre Dame*", Kiki jokes, as she discusses the shoulder pads that defined the female silhouette of the era. Jewellery followed this bold trend, and earrings were statement pieces, worn to stand out and leave an impression. The 80s saw the rise of costume jewellery, affordable pieces that could still make an impact. It was the era of individuality, of expression, and Kiki combined the daring of the 80s with the glamour and exclusivity expected from fine jewellery. Women were no longer simply turning to their granny's pearls anymore in this fashion-defining decade; they wanted pieces to express their own style. During this revolution, brands like Butler & Wilson became popular for their striking costume jewellery, but if someone wanted something finer there were only the likes of Cartier, Tiffany, and similarly expensive brands to choose from. Kiki noticed a gap in the market for pieces for around £500, and she set out to fill it.

"It was the era of individuality, of expression, and Kiki combined the daring of the 80s with the glamour and exclusivity expected from fine jewellery"

With her first collections, Kiki focused on heart, bow, and circle motifs, creating pieces in both 9ct and 18ct yellow gold. Her original stones of choice were very different to the colourful gemstones associated with the brand today; rock crystal, agate, haematite, lapis lazuli, and black onyx. Whilst her designs were bold in size and shape, Kiki opted for muted colours, pieces that could be worn with a power suit at work and add to the purpose of the outfit, not fight it for attention. These were gemstones she had seen and loved in her father's shop, set in pieces from throughout the decades, but they were too large and 'of their time' to wear as everyday jewellery. Only six months later, she started working with citrine and amethyst for a more varied colour palette, other gems she had seen in her father's shop which provided a fun pop of colour. These colourful stones spoke to the modern woman; more affordable, less readily available in the luxury market, and a refreshing change from the sapphires, emeralds, and rubies that clogged up the windows of their favourite jewellers. As a result, Kiki became an integral part of the jewellery zeitgeist at the time. This first collection was the beginning of Kiki's love affair with gemstones and what they could do, a love that would continue over forty years and still thrives to this day.

MAKING MONEY
LIKE MEN

Towards the end of the 80s, Kiki began to see the changes in consumer buying habits. Traditionally, fine jewellery was selected by a gentleman and presented to his wife or lover as a gift. This slowly changed, and women would come into the store with their husbands so they could choose a piece together. Not long after, women visited the store alone and made their selection, then told their husbands who would subsequentially drop by and make the purchase. But the latter half of the 80s, and every decade since, has seen women coming into the store to make purchases for themselves. The 80s saw a boom in working women with autonomy, finally seeing themselves in positions of power, and making money like men. Not only was there a female Prime Minister leading the country, there was also a successful feminist movement and advancement in workplace equality, resulting in a long-awaited societal shift. Women finally had disposable income and wanted to spend it, and jewellery was the perfect indulgence. The gemstones at Kiki McDonough were colourful and expressive and more affordable than high-end jewellery houses, so buying something for oneself did not come at an extortionate cost. With Kiki at the helm, customers could be assured that the jewellery they were buying was stylish and functional, made by a woman for women. And, not only did fine jewellery act as a stylish accessory, it was also an investment with re-sale value, unlike the expensive clothing to which women were also turning with their salaries. Kiki's gap in the market was proving a big success.

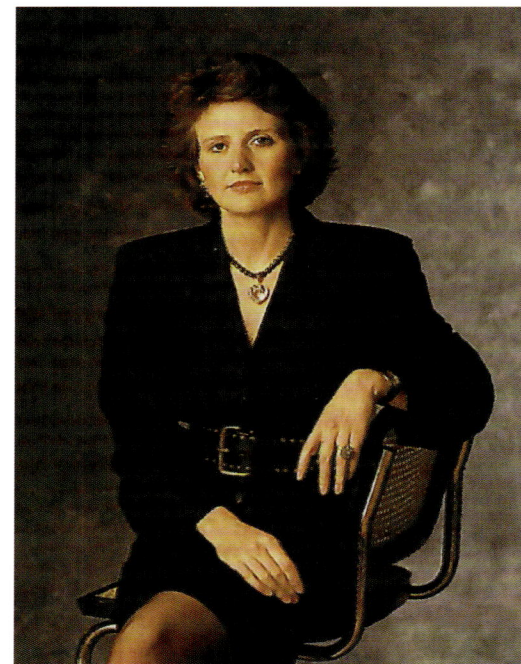

Kiki in 1989

Kiki spent three years at Nigel Milne's store and expanded her range there, culminating in many more pieces and a circle of dedicated clients. Most of the women Kiki found herself getting to know had only worn pearls and a minimal amount of costume jewellery before shopping at Kiki's concession, so they began to slowly build up a collection of wearable fine jewellery that didn't need to be saved for a special occasion. In 1986, a necklace was featured on the second page of Vogue, the first ever piece of Kiki jewellery published anywhere, putting Kiki McDonough on the map.

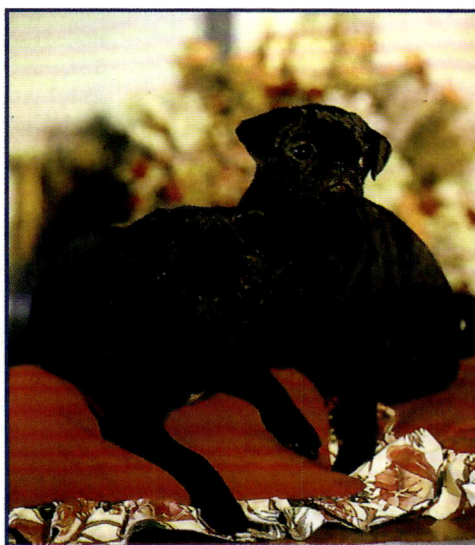

Florence introduces Siena to her favourite jewellery

KIKI McDONOUGH

AT

NIGEL MILNE LTD.

MODERN **JEWELLERY**

16C GRÁFTON STREET, LONDON W1X 3LF TEL. 01-409 0255

Kiki's pugs Florence and Siena featured on an early Kiki McDonough brochure

Haematite necklace in 9ct gold with Russian wedding ring rondels

Pearl and haematite earrings in 9ct gold

THE FIRST STORE

In 1988, Kiki moved her now-established brand to her first stand-alone store on Elizabeth Street, Belgravia. The opportunity came about when David McDonough had lunch with a friend who mentioned a small store attached to his house, and he jumped at the chance for Kiki. Moving away from a concession format and occupying a space on her own was a big leap, and the beginning of an exciting adventure for the brand. Kiki wanted her store to be open and welcoming, somewhere people felt comfortable entering for a browse, a contrast to the shops she remembered visiting in the West End as a child.

"I look back now to all those jewellery shops in the West End when my father had his shop – it was burgundy velvet and dark mahogany wood, there were bells on the doors and men in suits descending on you as you walked in, and you never spoke above a hush – not my scene at all! It wasn't very conducive to what I thought retail should be."

An illustration of Kiki's first store on Elizabeth Street

After only a few days on Elizabeth Street, Kiki developed chicken pox, so her mother took over for two weeks and allowed the show to go on. *"I was so scared,"* Kiki says about the opening of this store, *"I thought 'what am I doing?'"*, but it turned out to be a good learning experience. The shop was small so the overheads were manageable, and this was an important factor in the success of the business, allowing Kiki to find and develop her brand and style without having to worry too much about the rent. *"The business has always been the thing that has pulled me to open a bigger store, and it has been nerve-wracking every time"*, Kiki explains, and she tentatively followed the brand that had somehow become bigger than anything she had ever expected.

> " *The business has always been the thing that has pulled me to open a bigger store, and it has been nerve-wracking every time* "

A selection of lapis lazuli, haematite, pearl, rock crystal, and chalcedony pieces from Kiki's 80s collections

A portrait of Kiki in the 1990s

1990s

A pair of fire opal and citrine Double Oval earrings in 18ct yellow gold

THE ART OF JUGGLING

A decade to remember, Kiki gave birth to her two sons, William and Edward. Raising children whilst running a business remains a struggle for any woman attempting to do both. It raises the age-old question, "*Can women really have it all?*". One look at Kiki, and you would assume yes. One of her mantras in life has always been: "*You can have it all, but not all the time*". Her secret? Juggling, and juggling well. It is a skill Kiki has had to master throughout her life – in 1991, Kiki and David got divorced (although he remained chairman of the business), she had a baby with her second husband, Randle, moved house, moved the location of her store to Walton Street, began preparing her business for a recession, and all in the space of 6 months. "*I used to go to bed with tears in my eyes wondering how I could possibly get up in the morning because I was so tired*", she states, but get up she did, and she is quick to praise the people who were around her for their help when she most needed it, especially her mother, whom Kiki fondly describes as having been "*above rubies*".

above: Kiki and her second husband, Randle Siddeley, at Albert Bridge

right: William, Kiki, Edward, and Randle at a party together

STARTING A FAMILY

above: a young William and Edward

above: William and Edward as children

above: William and Edward serving snacks at an event in Kiki's store on Walton Street

T he beginning of the 1990s saw one of the worst recessions in recent history, and Kiki felt the strain badly. With a two-year-old and a baby, a company, and a husband whose landscaping business was having a challenging time due to a lack of people purchasing property, she was exhausted. Seven days after her second son, Edward, was born, she was back in her store, determined to steer her business through the other end and desperate to keep the train on the track. It was, Kiki confesses, *"the hardest period of my life"*. It was due to her kind landlord and decent rent that the shop was able to keep going, and the family made it through the recession intact.

Kiki's children have always known the importance of what their mother did for a living, and Kiki involved them in the business as much as she could. *"I would bring them into the shop and show them a necklace and a pair of earrings and then I would go to them a couple of weeks later and say, 'You know that purple necklace I showed you, well, I sold it today!' and they would be so excited"*. She emphasises the importance of including her children in her business, so they always understood where she was, and where the money came from. Kiki would tell her boys that they would need to wait and see how the shop was doing before she could buy them a new tennis racket or pair of trainers. There was always an element of guilt, because there are so many events and activities in a child's life and a business owner cannot be there for all of them, but when Kiki expressed this concern to Mrs A, she was told to *"stop being so neurotic!"*, and understood that doing her best was often good enough. Though showing up for her children would take priority, Kiki knew that missing a couple of school fetes, or the dreaded easter bonnet parade, would not ruin her sons' lives, and she was always there for the important stuff. Her sons scarcely remember the details of those early days, and after asking William if he remembers his parents coming to watch a cricket match at Stowe, he fondly recalls them being too loud and embarrassing him. When William and Edward were children, Kiki never left the house before them in the morning, and this was non-negotiable. *"People used to ask me how many shops I had, and my answer was always the same – one shop and two children"*, Kiki says, and she will never regret spending as much time as possible with her boys rather than taking the company global earlier on.

"Kiki's children have always known the importance of what their mother did for a living"

As a mother, Kiki was practical and firm, but always ready to laugh with her sons. Sporty and energetic, William and Edward bounced around the house, kicking footballs through windows and always desperate to go to the park as soon as their parents were home from work. There seemed to be only one answer when they were young; a male nanny, and Vlado from Slovakia changed all of their lives. Soon the boys grew up and went off to boarding school, ready to tread their own paths. With a mother as pragmatic as Kiki, she made this path all the safer by arranging a safety and security talk with a former SAS officer at her house in Battersea with thirty of her children's friends (William remembers this vividly, and still gets teased about it now by his friends who were there). The boys developed personalities quite different from each other; William boisterous and outgoing, Edward curious and sensitive, both blessed with the famous Axford sense of humour. Kiki knew how important it was to rebel as a child, having spent her own childhood doing just that, so when she received a call from Edward's school two days before the end of his final year, telling her that her golden child had been suspended for drinking in a car park at midnight, her reaction was pure glee. She never had the same issue with William, who was always getting up to mischief.

"People used to ask me how many shops
I had, and my answer was always the same –
one shop and two children"

FOOTBALL FANATIC

It is her children Kiki has to thank for her love of Liverpool football club. After deciding to try and like football in order to connect with Edward whilst her eldest was at boarding school, her pretence quickly turned to enthusiasm, and a true Liverpool fan emerged. The most-watched channel in Kiki's house is Sky Sports, and Sundays are often spent shouting at the TV. If Kiki arrives at the office with a spring in her step, it is most likely because Liverpool have just won a big game. No wonder the fire opal gemstone is so prevalent in Kiki's collections when her chosen team play in red. Kiki now counts football as one of her greatest passions, alongside the ballet.

Kiki's beloved Liverpool Football Club shirt

THE 'KIKI GIRL'

With her business well and truly established, the 90s allowed Kiki to develop and strengthen her brand image. The ideal 'Kiki girl' is, according to Kiki, *"stylish, enjoys what she wears, but is not obsessed by fashion and the latest fads"*. In other words, Kiki's target customer is classic, polished, and not led by trends, very much like Kiki herself. Having built a brand which has always prided itself on creating classic pieces with a twist that can be passed down through the generations, Kiki's views on fashion are clearly reflected in her designs. She believes trends are for clothes and not for jewellery, so if you were to pick up an old Kiki McDonough catalogue from the 90s, several pieces will jump out at you from the page that you would want her to sell again. She describes her own style as *"neat and chic"*, clothes that look put-together but not overdone, that make her feel comfortable but appear polished, an image you must present if you want to be respected in the luxury sphere. As a result, her jewellery is not excessive and cutting-edge, but plays with simple shapes and wearable colours, her intention being that women should feel prettier with a pair of her earrings on than they did without. Earrings sit so close to a person's face that they can, with the right coloured gemstone, enhance and light up their features. Kiki notes her mother, Mrs A, as one of her style inspirations, and remembers fondly a brooch she used to wear, a citrine and amethyst four-leaf clover design with diamonds, and how it glinted on her sleeveless purple shift dress as she said goodnight to a young Kiki before heading out for the evening, kitten heels tapping on the floor, leaving the distinctive smell of Carven's 'Ma Griffe' lingering behind her. The brooch felt like the most important part of the outfit, elevating something simple and making it stylish and personal. That is what jewellery is supposed to do.

" My hectic lifestyle is one that is shared with many women and has contributed to how I design – my pieces have to go with everything and go everywhere."

Yvonne Axford's citrine, amethyst, and diamond clover brooch which Kiki fondly remembers from her childhood

Kiki's biggest thrill is seeing different women wear her jewellery. From the pavement of King's Road to the stands at a Liverpool match, glimpsing a Kiki McDonough design in public never gets old. Kiki has always maintained that her biggest source of inspiration is her customers and peers, and what better way to know what women want than by asking? Having built a rapport with her clients over the past decade, mostly by spending every day talking to them on the shop floor, Kiki could take what she learnt from them, what they looked for when they entered the store, which gemstones they bee-lined towards, and incorporated this into her designs moving forward. Whilst Kiki McDonough had been selling jewellery in sterling silver and 9ct gold throughout the 80s and 90s, it was 18ct gold that Kiki decided to focus on, her decision based on customer buying habits as well as on instinct. Her core gemstones – blue topaz, white topaz, green amethyst, amethyst, citrine, and peridot – became prevalent in all gemstone-based collections alongside rarer gems such as fire opal, green tourmaline, and morganite.

THE KIKI
BLUE & PURPLE

When deciding on updated brand colours after her move to Walton Street, Kiki, of course, turned to gemstones to guide her. The blue topaz and amethyst Double Oval earrings proved how well sky-blue and rich purple worked together, so a pair of these earrings became the inspiration for her branding. The colour blue represents loyalty and trust, whilst purple has connotations of luxury and royalty, so the combination of the two colours signifies luxury you can depend on, the backbone of Kiki McDonough. Since this brand update in the early 90s, every time a customer buys a piece of Kiki jewellery they will untie a purple satin ribbon and open the inviting light blue box, revealing their sparkling treasure inside.

opposite: A selection of garnet, pearl, agate, onyx, and carnelian pieces from Kiki's 80s collections

KIKI & THE ROYALS

The first British royal to wear Kiki McDonough, in 1986, was Sarah Ferguson, the Duchess of York. The Duchess arrived at Bordeaux airport positively glowing in onyx heart and bow earrings and a pearl and onyx crystal heart necklace. So began a relationship with the British royal family that would span generations and solidify Kiki as a jewellery designer fit for royalty. Not long after this first appearance, the late Diana, Princess of Wales, began to wear Kiki jewellery, and was photographed in a pair of Kiki earrings in 1990 on a state visit with First Lady, Barbara Bush. A style icon for many, Princess Diana's jewellery box was soon filled with Kiki designs, and the Kiki McDonough name was catapulted into the spotlight. Kiki fondly remembers the day Princess Diana visited her store in Elizabeth Street, how she was in the side kitchen making herself a cup of coffee before opening hours when a builder working at the shop next door informed Kiki that Princess Diana was tugging at the door handle to her shop. Kiki assumed he was joking, and it wasn't until the builder came to tell her for a second time, with a tone of urgency, that she believed him and went to the door. In came the princess herself, charming and demure, looking for a piece for her next event. To make a good situation even better, Kiki had gone for a drink with a gentleman a week beforehand and, when he inevitably asked her what she did for work, was unimpressed and uninterested when Kiki told him about her jewellery business. It was perfect timing, then, that this same gentleman happened to walk past the shop when the Princess of Wales herself was inside. Kiki acknowledges that this visit improved her credibility in the eyes of men who still doubted her, of which, even after years of success, there were a few. Kiki describes her relationship with the British royal family as *"a joy"* and never downplays the value of having a member of the Royal Household wear her designs, though she is discreet in mentioning her decades-long connection.

"Princess Diana's jewellery box
was soon filled with Kiki designs,
and the Kiki McDonough name was
catapulted into the spotlight"

HRH Princess Diana and First Lady Barbara Bush at the White House in 1990.
Princess Diana is wearing Kiki's iconic pearl, Russian wedding ring rondel, and amethyst earrings

DOUBLE OVALS

The early 90s produced one of the most timeless and memorable Kiki designs, the Double Ovals. These earrings were first inspired by the Spring Fairy costume in a performance of Sleeping Beauty at the Royal Opera House, a beautiful blue and green tutu which caught Kiki's keen eye from the audience and had her scribbling the colour combination on the back of her ballet programme. From this, the blue topaz and peridot Double Ovals were born, and it is a design that has remained as popular today as when it first launched. The rhyme *"blue and green should never be seen without a colour in between"* was a code by which the jewellery world lived in the 80s and 90s, but Kiki set out to dispel the myth. The original Double Ovals marked the beginning of Kiki's innovative colour combinations, and she started mixing all kinds of gemstones that other designers weren't even contemplating; the royal purple of amethyst with the golden orange of citrine, magenta pink rubellite with soft green amethyst, red fire opal with the summery grass green of peridot. In fact, many of these combinations were inspired by ballet costumes. If certain colours can be put together in clothes for great effect, why not jewellery? Perhaps Mrs A's citrine and amethyst brooch was Kiki's first inspiration for combining colour, something her mother had loved, something every woman would want. Kiki remembers the 90s as *"more adventurous* [than the 80s] *...people were a bit more receptive to colour"*, so this was the perfect time to start experimenting with gemstones.

"The original Double Ovals marked the beginning of Kiki's innovative colour combinations"

above: An illustration of the blue and green tutu that inspired the original blue topaz and peridot Double Oval earrings

left: The original blue topaz, peridot, and diamond Double Oval earrings, inspired by the Spring Fairy's tutu in Sleeping Beauty

top: A pair of peridot, morganite, and diamond Double Oval earrings in 18ct yellow gold

centre: A pair of lavender amethyst, iolite, and diamond Double Oval earrings in 18ct white gold

bottom: A pair of blue topaz, fire opal, and diamond Double Oval earrings in 18ct yellow gold

KIKI IN SOCIETY

There is something to be said for dressing for the life you want to live, and Kiki's life has been as colourful as her jewellery. Whilst working on growing her business, Kiki frequented the London social scene and became something of a socialite, often appearing in the glossy pages of Tatler magazine in her finest dress and Manolo heels with her second husband, Randle Siddeley. After marrying Randle, Kiki became Lady Kenilworth, a title that held more weight in the 90s than it does in the modern day. Today, you *"rightly have to earn respect"*, though Kiki believes that being a lady is a state of mind, rather than a title bestowed upon a person. Once, an acquaintance mentioned Kiki's title in a down-her-nose sort of way, but Kiki reminded her that she had always been a lady, her title was simply something she had gained through marriage, and proudly, as her husband's inventive and pioneering ancestor had earned it. Randle's great-great-grandfather, John Davenport Siddeley, started the Armstrong-Siddeley Car Company and received his peerage for important work in engineering, producing aircraft engines and ambulances during the First World War. The Siddeley family remained extremely successful and creative after John Siddeley passed away, and Randle is no exception with his eminent landscaping business.

Mail Diary

Secret's out: Randle and his love Kiki plan to marry

Calling their own bluff

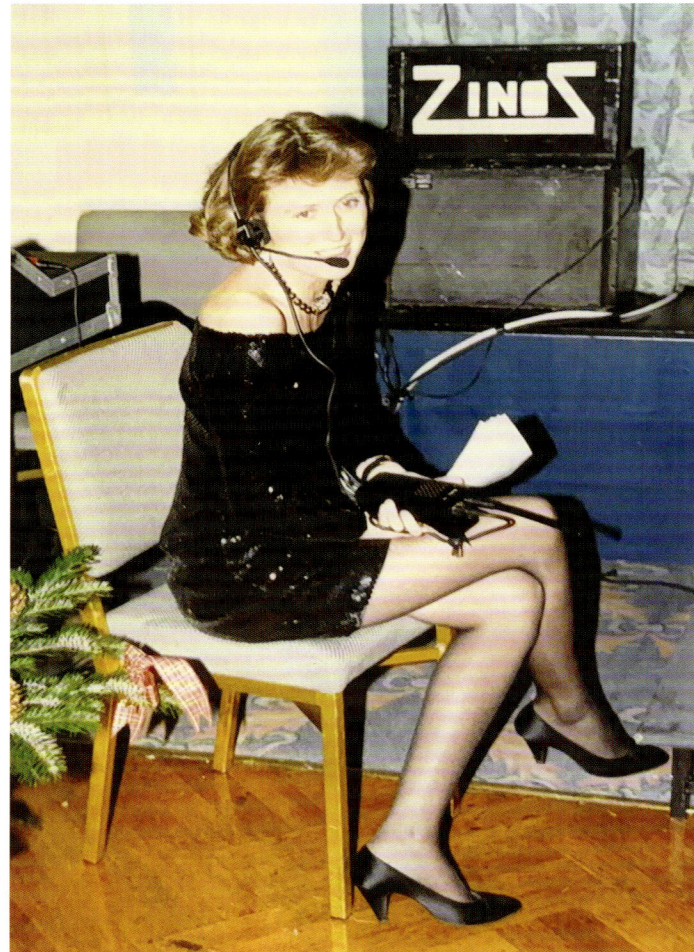

above: A newspaper article discussing Kiki and Randle's relationship. They had previously dispelled rumours of romance but the Daily Mail managed to get hold of the story anyway!

right: Kiki hosting a charity fashion show at The Savoy in 1990

Social stereotypes

By Victoria Mather. Illustration by Sue Macartney-Snape

The non-skier

When the alarm goes off at 7.30am and Kiki's husband stumbles out of bed with a raging hangover, cannot find his ski socks or his avalanche bleeper, and then keeps the ski guide waiting while he takes a call from Hong Kong on his mobile, Kiki just snuggles under the duvet and sleeps blissfully through the maelstrom taking place in the boot room. She certainly doesn't get up to check the children's ski passes – what else is Nanny Tracy for? When all have left, in a turmoil of clashing skis, to get the first lift, and an unnatural calm has descended on the chalet, Kiki will rise in a pale pink cashmere dressing-gown, make herself a cappuccino and have a leisurely bath in Dr Hauschka's Bain à la Lavande while skimming a Jackie Kennedy biography. She has gone to extravagant lengths to achieve this idle perfection: about four years ago she tweaked a ligament while skiing, an event which rapidly became 'ripping my entire knee out', so that any suggestion of risking the slopes is met with a brave smile and a sad shake of the head. To an audience ignorant of the tentative nature of her relationship with vertical snow, Kiki may murmur about how much she loved off-piste. Actually, off-piste to her is a street without shops. Now, swathed in furs and the softest leather boots, Kiki wafts. She wafts to the heavenly busy restaurant where everyone has agreed to meet for lunch – and when the skiers are late, repels boarders at her entirely empty table for 10 with a gimlet glance over the Versace sunglasses. She wafts to the manicurist, the spa and the coiffeur. She wafts, after a restorative hot chocolate and the purchase of yesterday's copy of *The Daily Telegraph*, to several achingly fashionable boutiques full of fluffy clothes you'd never ever wear outside a ski resort. She buys all of them – 'Darling, it comforts me so for not skiing.' If not busy having a siesta, Kiki might collect a child from the ice rink and purchase an amusing amount of foie gras, then book herself a treatment of being beaten with birch twigs soaked in rose water at the spa. By the end of the holiday she is rested, luminous, lightly tanned and has actually read *The Blind Assassin*. The keen skiing wives hate her.

above: A society page in The Telegraph – 'The Non-Skier' was based on a conversation Kiki had in the mountains with Victoria Mather about her disinterest in the sport which led to this parody

right: Kiki featured in a newspaper article in the 90s

Kiki McDonough

Society jewellery designer *(see A Girl's Best Friend in this issue)* Kiki says, 'I've always believed that the chicest woman in any room is the one who is wearing the simplest outfit. When customers come to me they need to feel confident about my own taste. I feel as though I can cope with anything when I'm wearing an Armani suit.' She wears the latest addition to her ever-expanding Armani wardrobe, a tailored black wool double-breasted coatdress, £895, from this autumn's collection. 'I wear it over a slim black skirt and T-shirt in my Walton Street shop during the day and then on its own for going out to dinner straight from work—and it's a perfect foil for my gold rope jewellery.'

After their marriage, Kiki and Randle became the couple of the moment, and the events and parties they were invited to as Lord and Lady Kenilworth were, to Kiki and her exceptionally social nature, an entertaining addition to their relationship. Credited with *"the best legs in town"* by Tatler after being photographed in a mini dress, Kiki's outfits, and most importantly her jewellery, was being looked at. *"It was great fun"*, Kiki recalls; she loved meeting new people, going to parties and socialising, but she made sure to never lose sight of the person she was when she started. Today, we may call her an 'influencer', (Tatler prides itself on being the original social media, after all), but Kiki knew the value of this constant socialising and the impact it had in promoting her business. She would spend her evenings wearing her designs to parties in the company of people who could afford them, discussing gemstones in a low-lit ballroom or at lunch over a glass of diet coke (her favourite drink), spreading the word the old-fashioned way. Before the age of social media and free advertising, it fell on business owners to do what they could to spread word of their brand, and what better way to do that than at busy events and in the society pages? *"The only way you could get your business out there was to be seen"*, Kiki states, and she was the kind of person who felt as comfortable being *"seen"* as she did sitting behind a shop counter. There was the risk that being in the pages of Tatler could take away from the credibility of the brand, but Kiki has never pretended to be anyone that she is not. As a result, Kiki's shop was soon known amongst her friends as the place husbands went to find gifts for their wives, and the place women went to browse beautiful pieces and spend money on themselves.

Two of Kiki's friends participating in a charity fashion show that Kiki hosted at the Savoy in 1990

A WOMAN
IN A MAN'S WORLD

Though society was changing and successful women were becoming more commonplace, it was still not easy to convince everyone of the brand's success. Kiki remembers an exchange with a man at Barclays Bank who, when she went to see him about her small overdraft facility, told her he didn't think they were the right bank for her, despite the business doing well at the time. It was "*definitely because I was a woman*", Kiki says, and she walked out without looking back and switched to HSBC Bank immediately. Being a woman in the business world is something about which Kiki has never complained, though she does acknowledge that it has been harder for her than it ever would have been for a man. It has made her more determined, because "*if you spend too long worrying about things like that it will hold you back*". That being said, she does think that being a woman has had its benefits, and using charm for the good of her business has come in handy over the past forty years. "*God gave us feminine wiles,*" she says, "*so I have no compunction at all in using them!*" However, her outlook on running her own business involves so many other things; discipline, being good to her suppliers (many of whom she has worked with for around twenty-five years), discretion, and the ability to see the funny side when things inevitably go wrong.

" God gave us feminine wiles,
so I have no compunction at all
in using them!"

A selection of Kiki's favourite gemstones in a variety of shapes and cuts

KIKI'S
GEMSTONES

Gemstones have been around since the beginning of civilisation, worn to denote status, used as talismans, and trusted throughout the ages to represent events of significance. Gemstones will outlive us all, and there is something magical about the way these vibrant treasures are carved into history. Cherished for centuries all over the world, gemstones are an intrinsic link between generations, a window into the past and a promise for the future. Whilst many things change over time, jewellery and gemstones remain intertwined in the multi-faceted story of humanity. When Kiki first started the brand, she gave herself the goal of introducing a different gemstone to the business each year, and this has led to an array of beautiful gems being featured in her collections. From popular quartz and topaz to rare tanzanite and fire opal, each stone has a rich history, and being the custodians of earth's small miracles is a responsibility the Kiki McDonough team takes very seriously.

Amethyst jewellery set in 18ct white gold from the Signatures collection

AMETHYST
A Royal Favourite

Kiki's 1980s collections saw the introduction of amethyst as one of her core gemstones. Highly prized throughout history, this striking purple variety of quartz was named from the Greek word *ametusthos* which means 'not intoxicated'. Thought to prevent over-indulgence and drunkenness, wine-loving ancient Greeks would drink out of cups adorned with amethyst and wear the stone as amulets around their necks to appease Dionysus, god of wine and pleasure. Once considered equal in value to diamonds, amethyst was worn in the Middle Ages by the English aristocracy to signify their royal status, and was championed in Russia by Catherine the Great. Due to its connection with royalty, amethyst can be found in many spectacular pieces in the jewellery archives of the British Royal Family. Having briefly fallen out of fashion in the 20th century, Kiki felt certain that *"this versatile stone [would] once again be popular and fashionable"*. Her first amethyst pieces included cabochon heart-shaped stud earrings set in 9ct yellow gold and a beaded amethyst necklace with an amethyst, diamond, and pearl pendant. Kiki's claim proved correct, and amethyst has continued to be one of her bestselling stones.

*"Amethyst always reminds me of
my mother and her beautiful brooch"*

A pair of amethyst and diamond earrings in 18ct white gold from the 2022 Kiki Uniques collection

BLUE TOPAZ
Something Blue

Kiki introduced blue topaz in the 90s, and this has become arguably her most popular gemstone. A soft sky-blue hue is her chosen colour, though topaz comes in countless colours and shades including yellow, pink, pale green, and red. Topaz was first discovered by Romans on the island once known as Topazios in the Red Sea. Due to generous rough deposits in Brazil, blue topaz was looked upon to cure illnesses by South American tribes, and in the Middle Ages, it was thought to break curses. Blue topaz is said to aid communication and improve wisdom, and, at Kiki McDonough, the light-blue hue is associated with our brides' 'something blue.' A gemstone which allows for a subtle pop of colour without drawing too much attention, blue topaz has become the ideal choice for Kiki's customers and can be found in every core gemstone collection. It suits most skin tones, and looks wonderful in both yellow and white gold.

" The pale blue of blue topaz is gentle, feminine, and suits every colouring"

above: An emerald-cut blue topaz cocktail ring from the 2023 Jazz collection
top right: A pair of blue topaz and diamond detachable earrings set in 18ct yellow gold
bottom right: A blue topaz and fire opal trilogy ring in 18ct yellow gold from the Forget-Me-Not collection

opposite: A pair of blue topaz and diamond detail earrings in 18ct white gold from the Kiki Diamonds collection

MORGANITE
Tickled Pink

"My favourite shade of morganite is, of course, the beautiful, pale, ballet pink"

Discovered in Madagascar in the 1900s, morganite is the pink variety of beryl and was baptised 'morganite' by Tiffany & Co's chief gemmologist George F. Kunz in honour of financier J.P. Morgan. Morgan was a gemstone enthusiast and avid gem collector, and a great customer of Tiffany & Co. at the time, where most morganite jewellery was sold. The gemstone comes in a variety of pinks, ranging from an almost colourless lilac pink to an intense salmon hue. Its pink colour has cemented morganite's place as the gemstone of unconditional love, and it is said to strengthen the emotion and help heal previous hurt. One of the most challenging gemstones to source, especially with a strong pink colour, morganite is popular in Kiki's *Special Editions* collections.

opposite: Jemima Jones in a morganite, yellow beryl, and diamond collar necklace, and Grace morganite and diamond stud earrings, from the 2017 Special Editions campaign

above: Pear-cut morganite and diamond earrings in 18ct white gold from the 2025 Petals collection

right: A 2023 Special Editions ring featuring a cushion morganite gemstone, surrounded by pear-cut diamond detailing, and set in 18ct white gold

CITRINE
The Sunshine Stone

The colour of summer, citrine is the yellow variety of quartz and comes in shades ranging from pale yellow to a dark, golden syrup colour, the latter earning the trade name *madeira citrine* due to its resemblance to the Portuguese dessert wine. A gemstone which looks as if the sun is bursting through it, citrine holds good energy and is thought to attract prosperity and success. Adored throughout the years, citrine was believed to protect people against evil thoughts by ancient Romans and was once referred to as the 'money stone' due to its supposed link with acquiring wealth. This gemstone was so much loved by Queen Victoria that not only did she wear citrine jewellery but also used the gem to decorate her and Prince Albert's summer residence.

*"I always say this gemstone
is liquid gold"*

*Citrine flower earrings with 18ct gold rope detailing
from the Florence collection, first released in 2017*

*A cross-style pendant spotlighting citrine and surrounded by
lavender amethysts, blue topaz, peridot, and diamonds in 18ct yellow gold*

PERIDOT
The Lost Gemstone

Favoured by Cleopatra, the famed queen of Egypt, peridot is a captivating olive green and is a gem variety of the mineral olivine. Steadily growing in popularity and increasingly becoming evermore expensive, this gemstone was originally discovered on the island of Zabargad in the Red Sea and was forgotten for centuries before being discovered again in the early 1900s. Thought to cleanse the mind and promote peace and compassion, peridot's yellow-toned green colour is reminiscent of a well-groomed lawn in summer, and the Egyptians aptly referred to it as the 'gem of the sun'. Traces of peridot have even been discovered in stardust, a fascinating remnant of the birth of our solar system dating back 4.6 billion years, making this gemstone a truly otherworldly choice for jewellery designers. Peridot has been used by Kiki for decades as one of her core gems, and she has claimed it as one of her favourite gemstones of all time, though it is now in the same league as morganite and fire opal in terms of its value.

" Peridot was so difficult to sell in the 90s, but around 2008, jade became expensive and the Chinese market, who adore green, started buying peridot. After this, it became more and more popular and expensive "

top to bottom:
A pair of peridot and diamond earrings set in 18ct yellow gold from the 2022 Kiki Uniques collection

A pair of oval peridot gemstones are encased in diamond-set zig-zags and complemented by round-cut mandarin garnets, from the 2023 Special Editions collection

Loose peridot gemstones

This bulbous cocktail ring from the Jazz collection is set with peridots and diamonds in 18ct yellow gold

LEMON QUARTZ
SMOKY QUARTZ
Enchanted Ice

A stone that is associated with happiness and communication, lemon quartz is actually a very light-yellow citrine. Quartz comes in many colours, from soft pink to smoky brown, and can be found all over the world. Due to its light-yellow hue, lemon quartz is said to improve clarity and reduce anxiety. The darker-hued smoky quartz is a gem with a strong connection to Scottish folklore and was thought to hold the power of the Earth Gods by Druids due to its earthy-brown colour. A gemstone with a rich history, Ancient Greeks believed quartz was ice that never melted because it was formed by the gods. They called quartz *krustallos*, which is where the word 'crystal' is derived from. The perfect stone for those who love subtle colours.

"Smoky quartz is the darkest stone we use, as it is softer than black, but just as wearable"

A pair of smoky quartz and lemon quartz earrings, set in 18ct yellow gold with diamond halos

KIKI McDONOUGH – A LIFE OF COLOUR

TANZANITE
The Special Occasion Gem

When Kiki married her second husband, Randle Siddeley, she opted for a tanzanite engagement ring. A gemstone so rare it can only be found in Tanzania, this gem was named tanzanite by Tiffany & Co. after its country of discovery in the foothills of Mount Kilimanjaro. The gem was only discovered in 1967, making it a very recent gemmological discovery, and a top-quality tanzanite can rival the deep blue of prized sapphires. In the short time since its discovery, tanzanite has risen in popularity, and was assigned the birthstone of December in 2002. A gemstone with a stunning blue-violet hue, depending on the direction through which it is viewed, the indigo variety of zoisite will display either blue, reddish-purple, or an undesirable green-toned yellow. This phenomenon is called pleochroism (Greek etymology, many colours) and, given there are 3 chromatic options, this type of pleochroism is called trichroism. This striking gemstone promotes inner strength and allows for a strong connection to creativity. Tanzanite can be found in Kiki's *Special Editions* pieces, and, when paired with white gold and diamonds, is a gemstone destined for the most special of occasions.

" My favourite tanzanites are those
with a hint of purple"

opposite top: This model is wearing Special Editions tanzanite and diamond earrings and a Special Editions tanzanite and diamond ring

opposite bottom: Kiki's tanzanite and diamond engagement ring, given to her by Randle Siddeley

IOLITE
The Compass Stone

According to legend, thin pieces of iolite were used by Vikings as filters to locate the sun on cloudy days, helping identify their location on ships in stormy seas, making this the stone of journey and creativity. Another trichroic gemstone, iolite will display blue from one direction, purple from another and brownish grey from the other. Often misidentified as tanzanite, iolite has also been named the 'water sapphire', and takes its name from the Greek word *los* which means violet.

> *" I love to wear navy, so iolite goes perfectly.*
> *I think it is a prettier stone than sapphire,*
> *provided it has a slight purple tint "*

above left: This Kiki Classics ring features a central iolite flanked by two lavender amethysts, set in 18ct white gold with diamonds

above right: These cushion-cut iolites are surrounded by diamonds and set in 18ct white gold

AQUAMARINE
Mermaid's Treasure

" The sea-blue colour of aquamarine is reminiscent of warm weather and clear seas "

A gemstone which embodies the gentle blue hue of the sea in summer, aquamarine was used as a talisman to protect sailors in ancient times from treacherous maritime journeys, and was thought to be the treasure of mermaids. It is a stone which appears to encapsulate the power and beauty of the ocean and the many mysteries within it. The blue variety of beryl, aquamarine's name is derived from two Latin words – *aqua* and *marina* – meaning 'water of the sea'. In Greek mythology, aquamarine belonged to sirens: evil mermaid-like creatures who would seduce sailors and lure them to their deaths. In the Middle Ages, aquamarine was thought to purify liquids and was sought after by monarchs at risk of being poisoned. Queen Elizabeth II's famous aquamarine parure was gifted to her upon her coronation by the president of Brazil, and with every state visit afterwards, more aquamarines were gifted and added to her collection. In Brazil, the deepest and clearest aquamarines have historically been sourced from the Santa Maria mine, though this mine has now been exhausted, and around the world, other mines compare their finest rough to the Santa Maria blue. In the modern day, aquamarine is looked upon to bring harmony and happiness to a marriage.

above: A vibrant blue aquamarine gemstone sits within two halos of brilliant-cut diamonds in this ring from the 2024 Special Editions collection

right: These aquamarine drop earrings were designed to mimic the motion of the sea, featuring briolette-cut pears that trickle down into a statement pear drop, and complemented by brilliant diamonds

top left: Loose green tourmaline gemstones
top right: This ring features a vibrant rubellite surrounded by 18ct yellow gold petal detailing and diamonds
centre: A cabochon cut green tourmaline cross with 18ct yellow gold and diamond detailing
from the 2023 Special Editions collection

TOURMALINE
The Rainbow Stone

" I love the soft, lighter green colour of tourmaline. It is so flattering and brightens up a person's features "

Tourmalines come in all colours of the rainbow, which is why they are so loved by jewellery designers. This gemstone has been used for centuries, but before tourmaline was discovered, it was mistaken for other coloured gems. The first recorded discovery of tourmaline was in Brazil in the 1500s, where a vibrant green gemstone was mistaken for an emerald. Many red gemstones in the Russian Crown Jewels from the 17th century, once thought to be rubies, are in fact red-hued tourmalines. It is the stone of art and creativity, collected by Shakespeare, and was used as a talisman by writers and artists from the Renaissance through to the Victorian Age. Rubellite is the trade name given to dark pink and red tourmalines, and can be found in a selection of Kiki's designs. Kiki McDonough's *Special Editions* collection boasts various shades of tourmaline including green, pink, and blue. A gemstone which promotes inspiration and self-confidence, tourmaline is thought to be a physical bridge to the spiritual world.

above: These striking Kiki Diamonds earrings feature green tourmalines and sparkling diamonds

right: Green tourmaline and diamond detail earrings from the 2024 Special Editions collection

FIRE OPAL
Playing with Fire

Named for their fiery orange-red hue, fire opals are gemstones that make a mark. Kiki first introduced fire opals in her 2014 collection *Playing with Fire*, and they have since become a favourite of the brand. Sourced from Mexico, fire opals are said to intensify the passionate feeling of love and promote inner peace. Opals have been adored for centuries, the kaleidoscopic colours that can be found in this gemstone so captivating that Arabic legend claimed opals fell from heaven in flashes of lightning, and Ancient Greeks believed they bestowed the gift of prophecy. Opals have even been said to maintain the colour and health of blonde hair. Though the fire opal variety doesn't display this rainbow of colours for which opals are known, they are still captivating in their own right. In true Kiki style, her first fire opal collection paired this blazing stone with other coloured gemstones such as blue topaz and pink tourmaline, creating striking pieces that promised to draw attention.

" I was one of the first people in the UK to use fire opal in my jewellery. The colour of this gemstone ranges from an orange colour to a deep red, and I think all hues are heaven "

above: This pendant from the 2024 Carousel collection features tapered baguette fire opals in shades ranging from vibrant orange to deep red

right: Fire opals are scattered throughout these statement diamond earrings from the Bubbles collection, inspired by the effervescence of champagne bubbles

A pair of fire opal and diamond earrings from the 2022 Special Editions collection designed to look like flames

GARNET
The Mummy's Charm

The name 'garnet' originates from the Latin *granatus*, which means 'pomegranate,' in reference to the deep red colour this stone shares with the delicious fruit. Worn and used throughout the centuries, garnet adorned the fingers of Ancient Romans in signet rings, the carved gem used to stamp the wax seals on their letters. They were also cherished by the Pharaohs of Ancient Egypt, with the gem often entombed with mummies as a charm for the afterlife. The famed philosopher, Plato, even had his portrait carved into a garnet. Whilst a deep red is the most commercially common hue of garnet, it can also be found in a wide variety of colours including the romantic purple-red of rhodolite garnet, the deep green of tsavorite garnet, and the citrusy orange of spessartine (or mandarin) garnet. Whilst all types of garnets share the same crystal structure, they can vary in chemical composition, and over twenty different species of garnet have been discovered. Worn as a talisman to protect the wearer against negative energy, the balancing and energising properties of garnet make this the perfect gemstone to represent the month of January and its new beginnings.

"Garnets are reminiscent of a sultry glass of claret, so why would you not like them? It is the January birthstone and needs to be in a modern setting to keep an up-to-date look"

right: A loose rhodolite garnet gemstone

opposite left: Captivating mandarin garnets hang from articulated diamond drops and are set in 18ct yellow gold

opposite right: This necklace from the Grace collection features a rich rhodolite garnet gemstone in a halo of diamonds, set in 18ct yellow gold

*" Diamonds are the perfect way to add glamour
to my everyday pieces, but I prefer them when
they are brightening the coloured gemstone "*

*These earrings are an explosion of brilliant-cut diamonds set in
18ct white gold, designed to commemorate the King's 2023 coronation*

DIAMOND
The Stone of Love

Diamonds are created by extreme heat and pressure that exists around a hundred miles beneath the earth's surface, and are the only gemstone which contain a single element: carbon. The word diamond comes from the Greek *adamas* meaning 'unconquerable' and 'indestructible'. It is the hardest stone known to man, fifty-eight times harder than any other naturally occurring material on the planet, and can only be scratched by another diamond. Mined and traded in India as far back as the 4th Century BC in the Golconda region, the fascination with diamonds then moved to Europe, where they became fashionable amongst European high society. Fifty light years away from Earth is a star called 'Lucy', a ten billion-trillion-trillion carat diamond, named after the Beatles song *Lucy in the Sky with Diamonds*, and is the largest natural diamond known to mankind. Beautiful and valuable, diamonds have been popular for thousands of years and symbolise love, strength, and good fortune. The Ancient Romans believed that Cupid's bows were tipped with diamonds, and the connection between diamonds and love still thrives today in the gifting of diamonds for romantic occasions such as engagements and anniversaries. Often used as a glittering halo to coloured gems in Kiki McDonough designs, these sparkling stones accentuate the beauty of other gems whilst shining spectacularly on their own.

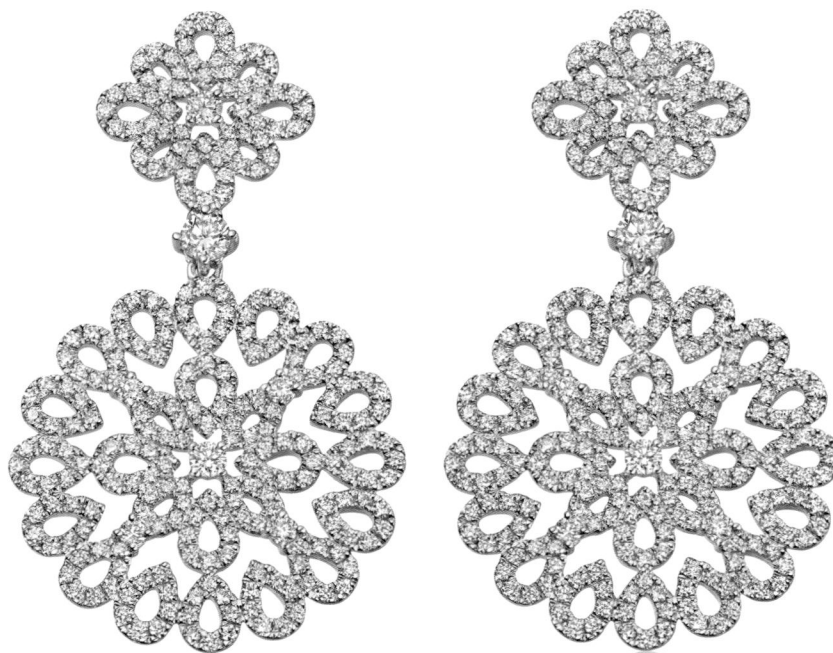

A pair of diamond earrings set in 18ct white gold from the Lace collection

HELIODOR

A Gift From the Sun

A member of the beryl family, alongside emerald, morganite, and aquamarine, any yellow variety of beryl is known as heliodor. A gemstone which takes its name from the Greek word *helios*, meaning sun, and *doron*, meaning gift, radiant heliodor aptly translates to 'a gift from the sun'. Although heliodor is one of the more commonly found beryl varieties, it is a lesser-known member of a commercially successful family. Representing generosity, power, and hope, helidor was first used to name a yellow-hued beryl in the early twentieth century. Helidor is often used in Kiki McDonough's *Special Editions* collections, the golden gemstone glowing like the sun after which it was named when set in 18ct yellow gold and paired with glistening diamonds.

" Heliodor has a slightly different hue to lemon quartz and citrine, but is equally as beautiful"

above: Delicate diamond-set loops wrap around the corners of this yellow beryl gemstone set in 18ct yellow gold

left: Square step-cut yellow beryls are surrounded by diamonds in these earrings from the 2022 Special Editions collection

PEARLS
An Oceanic Prize

The first mention of pearls dates back to a Chinese historian in 2206 BC, and they have been loved and worn for centuries since. Formed inside a mollusc when they produce a substance called nacre around an irritant (usually a parasite or a grain of sand), pearls can be both natural (when this process happens in nature without human intervention) or cultured (in a pearl farm with human intervention). Greek mythology associated the iridescent white of pearls with love and marriage, believing they could bring harmony to relationships. In Ancient Rome, pearls symbolised wealth and status, the precious oceanic creation prized and loved above most gemstones. Today, pearl jewellery is still extremely popular. Often worn by brides and passed down by mothers and grandmothers for the special day, pearls have conventionally represented purity and innocence. Whilst they have come to mean something different in the modern age, the tradition of wearing pearls has not dated.

Three pairs of pearl earrings with various diamond motif tops set in 18ct white gold

LAPIS LAZULI
The Celestial Stone

A gemstone that has been treasured for thousands of years, lapis lazuli was mined in Northern Afghanistan as early as 7000 BC. An eye-catching royal blue colour, beautiful specks of pyrite create a distinctive gold sparkle and make for a celestial effect. Highly prized and once valued as much as sapphires, many references to sapphires in the Bible are actually citing lapis lazuli. Originally traded in The Middle East and Afghanistan, lapis lazuli became popular in Europe in the Middle Ages, used in jewellery, sculptures, and ground down in pigment for artists. Michelangelo used this gemstone to create striking blue hues in his paintings, and Egyptian priests and royalty donned lapis lazuli-dyed garments to represent their God-like status. The famed explorer Marco Polo wrote about visiting the lapis lazuli mines in Afghanistan in 1271, though few other people have been able to make the treacherous journey to follow in his footsteps.

"Looking at this gemstone is like looking into a starry night sky"

Kiki Cushion lapis lazuli and diamond detachable earrings in 18ct yellow gold

"I love the bright green colour of malachite, and the rings that wrap around the stone make it so interesting to look at"

MALACHITE
Egyptian Protector

Kiki Cushion malachite and diamond detachable earrings in 18ct yellow gold

First used and traded in Egypt around 4000 BC, malachite was originally extracted from King Solomon's copper trading mines in the Red Sea, and gets its remarkable bright green colour from copper. A mineral which is created from a chemical reaction between already existing minerals, malachite displays beautiful light green rings, adding character and beauty to the stone. Known as the stone of guidance and protection, Ancient Egyptians would carve malachite into amulets to ward off evil spirits and, like lapis lazuli, it was used as a pigment in paint and make-up. Extremely popular with Russian royalty in the 19th Century, the famous Winter Palace in St Peterburg, Russia, contains the illustrious 'Malachite Room,' showcasing this vibrant gem in furniture, decorations, and pillars.

CARNELIAN
The Sunset Stone

The precursor to fire opal, a stone that would come to define the brand's use of vivid colour, carnelian played a big part in Kiki's jewellery designs in the late 80s and early 90s, sometimes paired with pearls and other gemstones, and always set in yellow gold. The orange-red variety of quartz, carnelian was an introduction to colour in Kiki's fine jewellery offering at a time when people were still wearing plain gold and a string of pearls. Still sold and loved forty years later, carnelian's distinctive colour sits proudly amongst the vibrant hues of Kiki's favourite gemstones. Easy to carve and originally turned into beads, intaglios, and cameos, carnelian has been referred to as 'the sunset stone' by gemstone lovers for many years, a nod to the fiery orange and red hues that make it so spectacular.

" I love carnelian for its orange-red colour
which I wear a lot in the summer"

above: These carnelian and pearl earrings first appeared in Kiki's collections in the 1990s

right: A Kiki Cushion carnelian and diamond pendant in18ct yellow gold

SAPPHIRE
The Sacred Stone

> *"I use colourful sapphires or blue sapphires mixed in with other stones to give them a more modern feel"*

above left: These statement curl earrings from the 2024 Carousel collection feature scattered irregular-cut sapphires in graduated orange and green tones

above right: This delicate bracelet features irregular multi-coloured sapphires and diamonds in 18ct yellow gold

Featured in the most famous ring in Britain, HRH Catherine Middleton's engagement ring that previously belonged to the late Princess Diana, sapphires have been linked to royalty for centuries. Sapphires belong to the mineral species corundum and have always been associated with a rich blue colour, though they come in a rainbow of colours, except red, as red corundum is known as 'ruby'. A gemstone that symbolises nobility and truth, the Middle Ages saw clerics wear sapphires to represent heaven, the midnight blue hue reminiscent of the sky above – a sky which Ancient Persians believed took its blue colour from a giant sapphire beneath the earth. Many myths and stories have been told about sapphires in the thousands of years since their discovery, the stone thought to have healing and protective powers, and the gemstone appears in the history and readings of several faiths including Christianity and Buddhism. Whilst sapphires make up one of the traditional 'big three' gemstones, fancy-coloured sapphires are encouraging contemporary jewellery designers to view the sacred gemstone in a new light, enabling sapphires to reach a modern audience.

Kiki McDonough Jewellery featured in 'Luxury London' magazine

2000s

A fire opal, lavender amethyst, and diamond bracelet from the Grace collection

An illustration of the distinctive King's Road street sign

THE KING'S ROAD

For Kiki growing up, the King's Road was something of a stylish wonderland. "*Chelsea was quite bohemian [back then]*", she says, "*the smart people lived in Mayfair and the West End*". The fashion world has a lot of history steeped in the red-brick buildings of King's Road; it is where the late fashion designer, Vivienne Westwood, chose to open her first boutique, where the late Mary Quant was inspired to design the miniskirt which defined 60s style, and, today, just round the corner on Symons Street, off Sloane Square, you can find Kiki McDonough's flagship store. At the centre of Chelsea life, Kiki's boutique is filled with sparkling gems and beautiful pieces that capture the eye of passers-by. The shop was not unfamiliar to Kiki, having once been her family butcher. The basement beneath the shop, now a charming office, was the cold storage for the meat. As soon as Kiki went to look at the shop on Symons Street as a potential location for her next move, she was convinced instantly. This aspirational new location, in Kiki's eyes, provided the brand with strong credibility, as Sloane Square is popular with tourists and Londoners alike for its stylish reputation. It was the biggest step in the history of Kiki McDonough, the shop much larger than those before, and the location steeped in Kiki's own history. Just across the road was where she began her first job at age sixteen, working behind the counter at Boots chemist, and the pavements are marked with seventy years' worth of her footsteps. As a teenager, Kiki and her friends would frequent the local pubs and a shop called 'The Stock Pot' where they could buy a bowl of spaghetti bolognese for about 75p. The famous road was more of a village, with fishmongers and bakeries standing where there are now fashion boutiques and Michelin-star restaurants. "*I don't look around and think about how so much has changed here since I was a child, it just seems too familiar*". For Kiki, opening this store was like coming home.

KIKI'S DETACHABLE DROPS

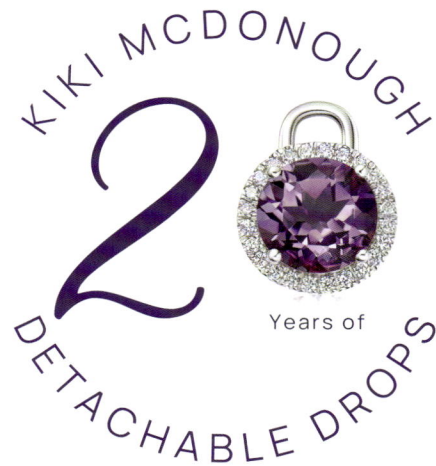

In 2004, Kiki released her first Detachable Drop earring collection. The idea of simple diamond hoop earrings with several attachments in different shapes and sizes meant customers could add to their collection, encouraging them to keep coming back. With the Detachable collection, Kiki considered the sociable working woman who would go straight from the office to dinner and drinks, her post-work ritual of quickly re-applying her make-up in the office bathroom elevated by adding a fun pair of drops to her work-appropriate diamond hoops, creating the perfect day to night transition. Having become known for her colourful earrings, this introduction marked the beginning of a brand-defining concept. According to Kiki, "*earrings should be the first piece of jewellery a woman should buy as they accessorise the face, adding light and accentuating features*", and earrings are what Kiki does best. Detachable earrings have become the bestselling category in the business, and the range is constantly being re-imagined and expanded. From classic cushion-cut gemstone drops to seasonal maple leaves, snowflakes and seashells, Kiki McDonough has a drop for every style and occasion.

" Earrings should be the first piece of jewellery a woman should buy as they accessorise the face, adding light and accentuating features"

top left: A logo designed in 2024 to mark 20 years of Detachable Drops in the company; an idea pioneered by Kiki as the ideal day-to-night earrings. This was celebrated by 20 pairs of Special Editions Detachable Drops in a ranbow of coloured gemstones.

above: An illustration of mandarin garnet and diamond drops, and an illlustration of amethyst and diamond drops

opposite: A selection of Kiki Hoops surrounded by Special Edition Detachable Drops in green tourmaline, peridot, yellow beryl, pink tourmaline, fire opal, rhodolite garnet, and diamonds

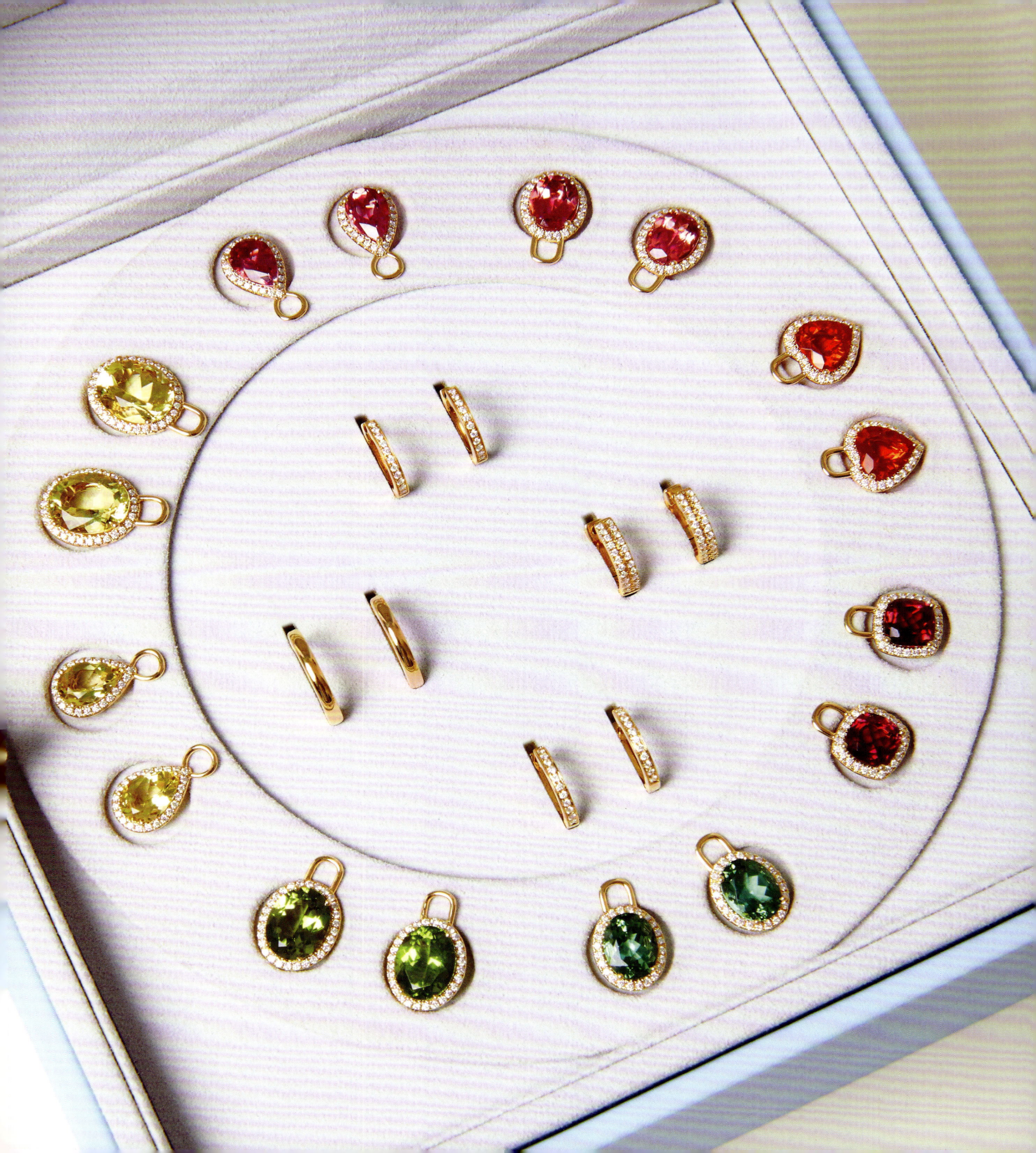

*Kiki double diamond hoops, pink tourmaline pear drops on Kiki classic hoops,
and green tourmaline oval drops on Kiki classic plain hoops*

top: Pearl and diamond detail cap drops in 18ct yellow gold

centre: Diamond snowflake drops in 18ct yellow gold

bottom: Rhodolite garnet and diamond drops in 18ct yellow gold

top left: *White topaz mosaic drops with a diamond accent in 18ct yellow gold*

top right: *Sunflower drops with a citrine centre and diamond accent in 18ct yellow gold*

bottom left: *Lavender amethyst mosaic drops in 18ct yellow gold*

bottom right: *Diamond petal drops with a peridot centre in 18ct yellow gold*

top left: Grace blue topaz and diamond drops in 18ct yellow gold

top right: Apollo fire opal and diamond drops in 18ct yellow gold

bottom left: Square step-cut peridot and diamond drops in 18ct yellow gold

bottom right: Blue topaz and peridot flower drops set in 18ct yellow gold

Kiki classic diamond hoops surrounded by oval lemon quartz and diamond drops, Kiki Cushion peridot drops, oval green amethyst and diamond drops, Kiki Cushion mini green amethyst and diamond drops, Grace peridot and diamond drops

Watermelon Tourmaline →

↖ *Diamond Halo*

Tanzanite ↘

Octagonal Cut →

Aquamarine ↘

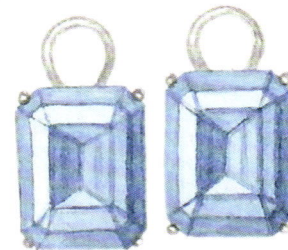

↖ *Claw Set*

Series of sketches illustrating: watermelon tourmaline and diamond drops; tanzanite and diamond drops; aquamarine drops

A 'RECESSION-PROOF' COLLECTION

Luckily, having gone through a recession eighteen years earlier, Kiki had some practice and resilince when another came along. Always keeping a firm eye on the newspapers, remaining alert to every headline, and everything that is said between the lines, is a vital skill when understanding how a business sits in an economic climate. "*If you run your own business, you'd be foolish not to read the papers and keep up with the news*", Kiki says, as anyone switched on enough can get a feeling from the page about which way things are going to go. Only a few months before the crash of 2008, someone approached Kiki about investing in her business, but she wasn't happy about the way the economy was going, and, after encouragement from Randle to trust her instincts (which have always proved reliable), she turned down the investment, a lucky save at the time as Lehmen Brothers bank went down only a month later.

Designing a 'recession-proof' collection was integral in keeping the business afloat, and so the Grace collection was introduced, named after the newborn daughter of a girl who worked at the store. Grace was designed to meet the demand for pieces with more accessible price points, with most pieces in the collection selling for under £1,000. Kiki's favourite coloured gemstones such as blue topaz, green amethyst, and citrine took centre stage in these understated designs, together with a subtle halo of diamonds. This collection first began with earrings and necklaces and has remained a bestseller ever since.

"If you run your own business,
you'd be foolish not to read the papers
and keep up with the news"

Grace blue topaz and diamond drops on Kiki double diamond hoops in 18ct yellow gold

above: Grace green amethyst and diamond necklace in 18ct yellow gold

opposite: Grace mini detachable earrings in citrine, lavender amethyst, and peridot with diamonds

THE BESPOKE JOURNEY

Jewellery tells a story: whether it has been handed down by a grandmother or purchased to mark a special occasion, a piece of jewellery will often hold a message or a memory that will be cherished for a lifetime. At Kiki McDonough, a bespoke design is a combination of our client's vision and our design team's skill, creating something truly remarkable. A bespoke piece can be commissioned by clients for many reasons: stand-out earrings for a bride, push presents for new and expecting mothers to one day hand down to their child, a statement ring to celebrate an anniversary. Whatever the reason for a personal piece of jewellery, the Kiki McDonough team is determined to exceed expectations.

The bespoke process begins with a client consultation where style, budget, gemstones, and function will be discussed. This brief is then passed from the retail team to the Kiki design team, who draw the design based on the client's wishes and start sourcing gemstone options. After the initial design is approved by Kiki, the client is shown the sketch, and any feedback or adjustments can be discussed. This process can be ongoing with much back and forth, but, eventually, the perfect piece will be created. Bespoke pieces can be commissioned for many reasons and hold an incredible amount of meaning. Some clients have come into the flagship store with old Kiki pieces they have been left by a beloved late family member and have had them re-imagined and reconstructed into jewellery that better suits their style. Other clients have pieces made to mark a special occasion such as a birthday, an anniversary, or an engagement. Fine jewellery is, and has been for many years, extremely personal, so the final product must be worthy of this sentiment.

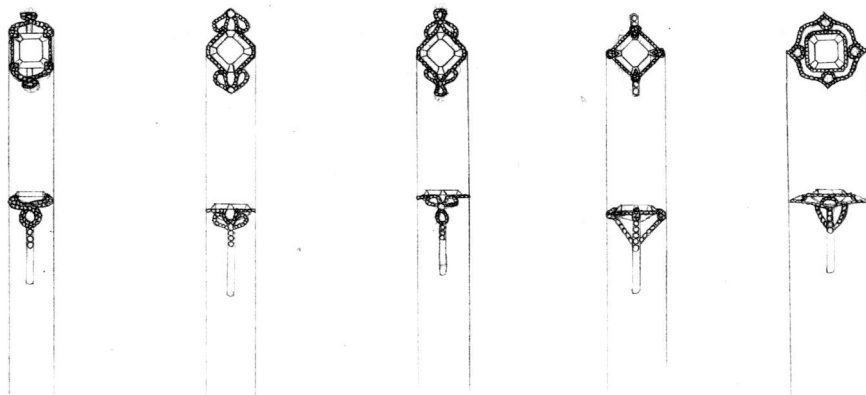

"Fine jewellery is extremely personal, so the final product must be worthy of this sentiment"

left: A selection of ring designs for a client who wished to re-model her engagement ring

opposite top: The creation of a Kiki piece inside one of the Kiki McDonough workshops

opposite bottom: The design stage of a pair of aquamarine and diamond earrings

40mm

- White Gold
- x2 Aquamarine Ovals - 13 x 11 - prong setting
- Diamonds 1mm round · microprong
- Post + butterfly

A pair of bespoke earrings featuring oval tanzanites, green tourmalines, and diamond accents set in 18ct white gold

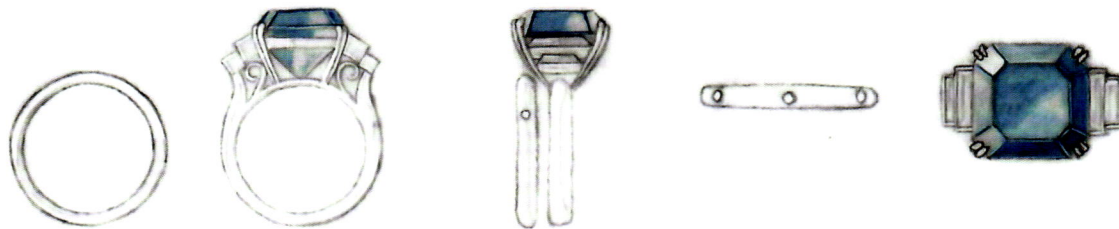

A 9.82-ct octagonal-cut aquamarine flanked by four baguette-cut diamonds set in platinum. This ring was created for a client who loved aquaramines and wanted a statement ring that would bring her joy every time she wore it

Three Special Edition cocktail rings in morganite, green tourmaline, and aquamarine

2010s

This Special Edition necklace features oval lavender amethyst and flower-shaped green amethyst gemstones

BRAND PARTNERSHIPS

This decade began with the opening of a Kiki McDonough concession in the renowned British lifestyle emporium, Fortnum & Mason, home to the very best of British, in the heart of London's Piccadilly. The first UK-based retailer to sell Kiki, this was an exciting opportunity for the brand to sit alongside other fine jewellers in this historic store. Fortnum's were the second wholesaler to stock Kiki McDonough, as only a year previous the brand had launched with the prominent US retailer, Niemen Marcus. This decade felt like the right time to start wholesaling, as the company was ready for a new challenge, and building these relationships meant an increase in both brand awareness and revenue. Kiki McDonough was expanding across the sea, and its dedicated US client base steadily growing. A decade later, in 2021, The Watches of Switzerland Group online, and select Mappin & Webb and Goldsmiths stores across the UK, welcomed Kiki McDonough, closely followed by Harrods, the famed luxury department store, in 2023. Seeing her designs in such prestigious retailers was a milestone for Kiki, and to become a part of their rich history was a privilege. Wholesaling has taken Kiki all over the UK, where she has talked at various locations about her journey as a luxury jeweller and subsequently discovered the most exciting part of any road trip: the Greggs sausage roll.

Kiki speaking at a Harper's Bazaar event in 2018

KIKI & THE BALLET

Kiki is known for her love of ballet. She was four years old when her mother first took her to a performance of *Sleeping Beauty*, and she was completely entranced, so a trip to the ballet became Kiki's yearly Christmas treat. Fast forward sixty-six years and the walls of Kiki's store are decorated with signed ballet shoes of past prima ballerinas, what free time she has is often spent at the Royal Opera House, and her patronages include the New English Ballet Theatre, a company founded to champion early-stage and developing ballerinas and choreographers. Hanging in the entrance of Kiki's store in Sloane Square is a pair of prima ballerina assoluta (the highest title given to a ballet dancer) Margot Fonteyn's ballet shoes, for which Kiki bid at an auction years ago. The shoes came with a letter, and this stated that the shoes were the pair Fonteyn had danced in during a performance of Giselle in 1964, which Kiki later realised she had seen as a child, finding her saved programme in a de-clutter years later. She also had a photograph of Fonteyn and Rudolph Nureyev dancing which she went to get re-framed and, upon looking at the back of the picture, realised that this too was from the same performance she had seen as a child. By sheer chance, the shoes, the programme, and the photograph all matched, and these are now three of Kiki's most prized possessions.

In 2015, the *Lauren Collection* was launched, inspired by prima ballerina Lauren Cuthbertson's performance in *Alice in Wonderland*. Kiki's friendship with Lauren began in 2011 when the two of them met after a performance at the Royal Opera House. Lauren was dancing *Manon* and, when the performance was over, Kiki asked Lauren to join her party for dinner, which turned out to be a success as the two of them got on splendidly. Their collection came to fruition a few years later when Lauren was injured during a performance of *Manon*. A piece of tape had been left on the stage when she was dancing and, in a pivotal moment when Lauren is pulled across the stage, her foot was caught, pulling all the tendons and forcing her out of action. After finding out about Lauren's injury, Kiki suggested they use Lauren's newfound free time to design a collection together, and what better way to celebrate a friendship? Many of Kiki's previous collections had been inspired by the ballet and the beautiful costumes on stage, so the introduction of *Lauren* continued the integral relationship between her designs and the arts. This collaboration resulted in a selection of delicate leaf motif designs adorned with diamonds, inspired by a house with leaves which appeared on the stage at the beginning of *Alice in Wonderland*. The ballet was written specifically for Lauren, so it seemed the perfect performance on which to base their collaborative designs. A collection as elegant as the ballerina after which it was named, the dainty leaves were a sparkling addition to Kiki's mostly gemstone-based jewellery.

"*My mother was so worried I was going to chatter all the way through* [my first ballet performance]. *But I didn't. I sat there, completely enraptured. I think my mother leaned over to say something to me and I told her to be quiet! I was only four and I was in my party dress. That was it. I've never looked back. I've still got the programme from that ballet*"

opposite top: An illustration of ballet dancers in motion

opposite bottom left: Diamond leaf earrings in 18ct yellow gold, inspired by Lauren Cuthbertson's performance in Alice in Wonderland

opposite bottom right: A pair of leaf motif earrings with diamond accents from the Lauren Collection

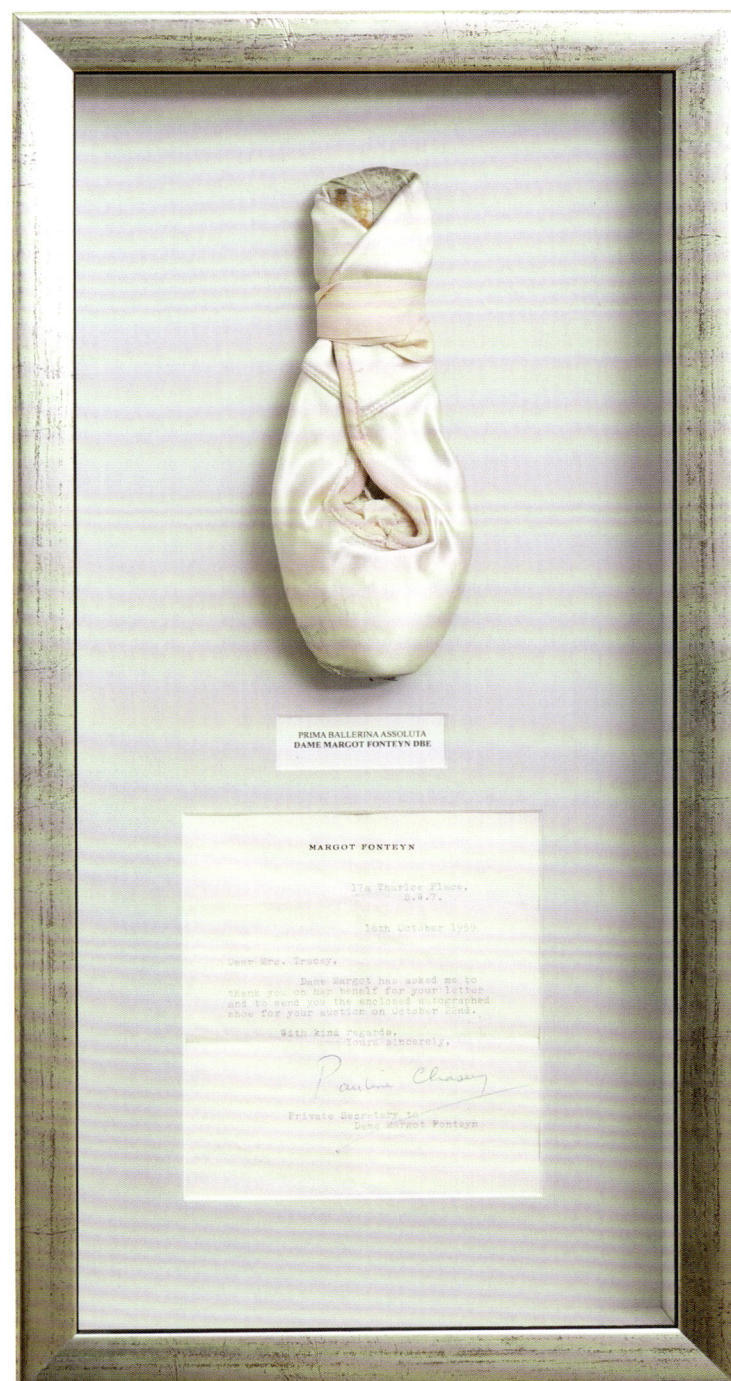

above: Kiki has treasured for years this Margot Fonteyn ballet shoe and the picture of Fonteyn and Rudolph Nuyeyev dancing Giselle in 1964

opposite: Lauren Cuthberson dancing in the 2020 brand campaign

KIKI McDONOUGH

CHELSEA IN BLOOM

A bustling neighbourhood with a vibrant heritage, Chelsea is the home of Chelsea in Bloom, a community event to coincide with the iconic Chelsea Flower Show. Every year the storefronts in the area are transformed into beautiful, themed floral displays, and Kiki never holds back. Ever since her marriage to Randle, Kiki has admired the artistry and talent that goes into creating a garden, so, of course, her display is always imaginative, drawing plenty of attention from the public. She has worked with florist Philip Corps several times on installations including an enormous octopus, a Jungle Book display featuring a giant Baloo and Shere Khan, and a cup of tea and steaming teapot, inspired by the theme 'British Icons.' Her first window in 2016 was a colourful archway based on the 'Rio' festival theme, featuring large floral replicas of Kiki's famous Double Oval earrings.

" Ever since her marriage to Randle, Kiki has admired the artistry and talent that goes into creating a garden"

An illustration of Kiki's 2023 Chelsea in Bloom display 'The Jungle Book' by Samantha Fleur Camp

A Chelsea in Bloom window inspired by Kiki in the 60s

A giant octopus wraps across the front of the shop during Chelsea Flower Show week

SPECIAL EDITIONS

After two decades of success with her collections, it was time to branch out to more exotic and lesser-known gemstones. Following on from the success of *Playing with Fire*, Kiki began a yearly *Special Editions* collection – exquisite designs created with rare gemstones of exceptional quality and cut. Fire opals have remained a firm favourite in the *Special Editions* collections alongside morganite, tourmaline, mandarin garnet, and other remarkable stones.

As these pieces are centred around beautiful gemstones, the design process usually begins with stone sourcing. Having met her main gemstone suppliers some 35 years ago at Basel Jewellery Show, Kiki's relationship with her suppliers is strong, and she sits with them, alongside the design team, to select the gemstones that captivate her the most. The chosen few are then the inspiration and basis for the collection's designs, which are hand-drawn and reworked several times before being computerised in CAD (computer-aided design) format. To check every element will work, a silver sample can be created from the CAD which is then wear-tested by the design team to ensure the design is flawless and the piece will sit properly when the stone is set in 18ct gold. Anything with which Kiki or her team are unhappy is altered on the design before the stones are sent to trusted craftsmen who expertly bring the pieces to life. When the sparkling jewellery arrives at the Kiki McDonough store, it is a thrilling affair for the team, who all fawn over the pieces like children on Christmas day. The design and production team sit together to carefully inspect every piece of jewellery for final quality control, and then the collection is hallmarked by the London Assay Office and ready to photograph. This process, from stone sourcing to the final product, takes months of work, but the end result is always worth it.

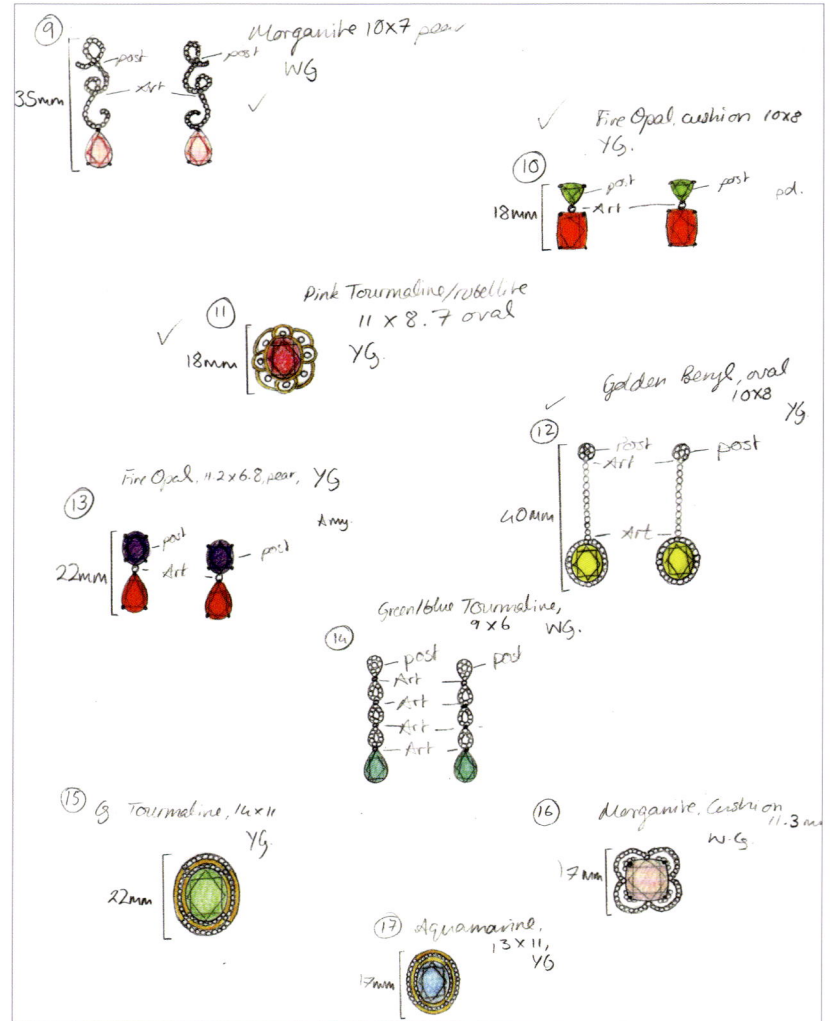

Sketches from the design stage of the 2023 Special Editions collection

" Four ballet-pink pear-cut morganites sit beneath cascading diamond ribbons in these charming earrings, and the bow detail at the top makes them even more exquisite"

" I love these flat-cut morganites with only the sides faceted, they merit having this exquisite diamond wrap detail caressing them "

" These earrings are perfect for special occasions, featuring icy green tourmaline gemstones in a trio of spectacular cuts, made even more special with their diamond halos "

"These asymmetrical earrings feature rich rubellites and beautiful green tourmalines, an unusual colour combination that enables both stones to shine"

"In these unique earrings, kite-cut beryls and tourmalines come together to create a striking celestial effect"

" The sparkling diamond detailing in these earrings is designed to mimic the facets of the central blue tourmaline gemstone "

" Blazing pear-cut fire opal gemstones sit beneath orange mandarin garnets for stylish earrings guaranteed to draw attention "

" This striking cross pendant features a beautiful combination of blue topaz, peridot, lemon quartz and diamonds "

" These elegant mandarin garnet and diamond garland earrings curl delicately around the ear "

LACE

Many of Kiki's collections have been designed with a nod to the nostalgia that memory inspires. The central motif for the Lace collection was inspired by Kiki's French grandmother's love of lace and an antique brooch of hers that had captivated Kiki as a child, the intricate diamond work reminiscent of hand-sewn French Chantilly lace. Like many children who admire the belongings of their grandparents, Kiki associates lace with fond memories from her childhood, visiting her grandmother's house in Normandy; the lace-trimmed tablecloths off which she would have her breakfast, the bedspreads she would curl up under, and, of course, the brooch that always caught her eye. This diamond collection is delicate and subtle with a slightly vintage feel; modern-day heirlooms inspired by the past.

" The central motif for the Lace collection was inspired by Kiki's French grandmother's love of lace"

opposite: Cressida Bonas wearing pieces from the Lace collection

right: A pair of diamond earrings in 18ct yellow gold from the Lace collection

MOVING INTO THE DIGITAL AGE

An exciting, and sometimes daunting, addition to the 2010s was the advent of social media. Navigating the world of the internet is the modern-day struggle nobody who began a business earlier than the 90s had foreseen, and it brought both challenges and high rewards. Kiki's citrine pear drop earrings flew off the shelves when Twitter (now known as X) first posted a picture of the then Catherine Middleton (HRH Princess of Wales) wearing them, with re-stocks selling out just as quickly for years afterwards. With information so readily available, people could buy the item they had seen and loved with a few clicks on their smartphone, making luxury accessible to a market which had otherwise been out of reach. As a direct result of the internet, customers all around the world could purchase Kiki McDonough pieces, and Kiki could easily receive widespread credit when public figures wore her designs. No need to pay £5 for a copy of the latest glossy magazine! As an increasing number of luxury brands found their clients shopping online rather than in-store, influenced by what they had seen on social media, the pressure to stay relevant and trendy is something many brands felt weighing heavily on their shoulders. This pressure has not eased with time. *"Ever since emails, anyone who runs a business is working 24/7"*, Kiki says, though she does force herself to put her phone down for an hour as soon as she gets home from work, a much-needed respite from the whirlwind of owning a business. *"It is a catch-22, the more you reply the more you get back, or the less you reply the more emails you have to answer!"*, though, she acknowledges, setting boundaries is important for living a life with some semblance of balance. Kiki has decided never to enter the world of social media herself, preferring to have her time online minimised as much as possible.

With computers becoming smarter, and design methods changing industry-wide, moving into the digital age also meant a change in design and production processes. Traditionally, Kiki would sketch her designs on paper and sit down with her craftsmen to discuss them, before the pieces were made in silver samples to check size and function. Before CAD was adopted, Kiki trusted in and relied upon her good relationship with her craftsmen for them to understand her, and produce something akin to the piece she had seen in her mind and sketched down. It was an in-depth collaborative process between designer and craftsmen, with both parties offering their skills and opinions. In the modern day, CAD is more efficient and cost-effective, with amendments quicker to make and ideas realised at speed, a process that links with the faster pace of modern-day consumerism. Whilst Kiki doesn't necessarily think that either past or present method is better than the other, this change in design and production means Kiki McDonough can release several collections each year and always offer customers something new. She does, however, state that her jewellery is not trend-led, so whilst new collections and memorable designs are important for relevance, the pieces the company creates should still be desirable and wearable in another forty years' time. For clients who spend thousands of pounds on jewellery, there must be a sense of thought and consideration in the creation of a piece, so whilst CAD has made processes easier, there is no less time and thought put into the original design than there was before the rise of the digital age.

Kiki jewellery featured in 'Country & Townhouse' magazine

'THE KATE EFFECT'

HRH Catherine, The Princess of Wales, has been a great help in the evolution of the brand. Whilst she wasn't the first royal to wear Kiki jewellery, she was the royal that coincided with the growth of online media. She subsequently became a modern trendsetter, with the British public and royal fans overseas waiting on tenterhooks to see what the young princess would wear to upcoming engagements. It is no secret that British businesses have had an uplift in sales whenever the Princess wears their product, the aptly coined 'Kate effect' working its magic, and Kiki often counts her lucky stars that she has been credited as one of the Princess's favourite jewellery designers. As the British Royal Family continue to strive for a more modern monarchy, it is no longer always appropriate for them to reach for the rubies and diamonds that fill the Royal Collection, so choosing a British brand that boasts timeless design and ease of wear as its selling point is a timely choice. Kiki's pieces are often seen complementing the princess's modest smile at events, she has sported multiple-coloured gemstones set in both white and yellow gold over the years, and it is a thrill for Kiki every time.

above: A pair of Signatures cushion and oval blue topaz and diamond earrings in 18ct white gold

opposite: Her Royal Highness Princess Catherine of Wales wearing Kiki McDonough blue topaz and diamond signature earrings

KIKI BRIDES

One of the main benefits of working in the jewellery industry are the precious moments of which you get to be a part. A regular stream of customers come into the Kiki McDonough store to purchase their wedding day jewellery, whether that be traditional pearls, their 'something blue', or a statement piece to elevate their white wedding dress. The Bridal offering at Kiki McDonough is always expanding, and Kiki has been fascinated by the iridescence of precious pearls for four decades.

" Getting married is such an exciting time. It is lovely for a bride to choose a special pair of earrings, a necklace, or bracelet to wear on their big day. However, I do think it is important for a bride to choose something they'll wear again, so that the memory of their special day can go on forever"

Kate Bulford wearing pearl and diamond Kiki earrings at her wedding

Abigail Saxon-Kitching with her husband Joe Kitching wearing Kiki cushion mini citrine and diamond detachable earrings

Tally Fosh wearing the Kiki Tiara at her wedding

Heart-shaped fire opal gemstones surrounded by diamonds on an 18ct yellow gold chain

FINDING LOVE IN SALINA

Kiki and Matthew at Kiki's 70th birthday dinner

In 2010, Kiki and Randle divorced amicably, remaining great friends and co-parents to their two boys. It wasn't until a few years later that Kiki found love again with British food writer and critic Matthew Fort. The two of them knew of the other but had never talked in depth, only brief "*hellos*" and the odd "*how are you?*", without ever caring much to listen to the answer, until a mutual friend's birthday dinner brought them together. Matthew was cooking fish, and Kiki brazenly requested the fish cheeks as she walked past him in the kitchen, which he saved and placed down in front of her at the table. After dinner, they sat beside each other in the sitting room (Kiki says he had no choice, there was only one free chair left in the room, next to Kiki, and Matthew came in last) and began discussing their plans for the summer. Matthew told her about a trip he was taking across Italy on a Vespa, tasting authentic Italian cuisine for a book he was writing called *Summer in the Islands*, and his excitement for the beautiful island of Salina, where capers are grown. Kiki told him it sounded wonderful, and that maybe she would come along for a part of it. He thought it was a great idea and a trip to Salina was the beginning of a slow-burn relationship. When Kiki asked her friend why on earth she hadn't introduced the two of them sooner, her reply was; "*Kiki, you dress in Prada, Matthew dresses in Orvis. On what planet would I think the two of you would get on?*" To which Kiki replied, "*I don't care if he dresses in Orvis, as long as I don't have to!*" There is always a smile on Kiki's face whenever she mentions Matthew, and when he drops into the store to visit her she can't help but grin like a schoolgirl. He does, of course, make her delicious food, and he makes her laugh. Both are as important as the other.

SEEING THE WORLD

An avid traveller, Kiki has been to all sorts of places, and a few of them have influenced her collections. Her Firefly collection was inspired by a trip to New Orleans with a friend in 1990, where Kiki watched in wonder as the fireflies danced across the calm surface of the Bayou, flashing in the twilight like embers from a fire. The motif of the firefly collection is a detailed diamond circle with a small gemstone glinting at its centre, a nod to the colourful lights emitted by these fascinating beetles. One of many trips around the world, Kiki is known to chase the sun, escaping the grey skies of London and jetting off for well-earned breaks on a far-flung beach somewhere. This love of sunshine inspired the Apollo collection, launched in 2017 and named after the mythological god of sun and light. The central motif of this collection features a glimmering circular gemstone encased in diamond-set rings and was designed to lighten up an outfit in the same way the sun can brighten a person's mood. Apollo still remains one of Kiki's all-time favourite collections.

Not only has travelling inspired Kiki's designs, but it has also influenced the way she views the world. When she was twenty, Kiki went hitchhiking around South Africa (something she would never encourage anyone to repeat!) and learnt the value of hard work. Her father gave her a return ticket, but Kiki had no money of her own, so had to earn her keep when she was out there. She found herself in a few positions, including waitressing in a steak bar and a rep job selling Pernod to different hotels. Her only worries were survival and having a good time, two life lessons she has carried with her to her seventies. Always one to accept a challenge, and hungry to experience all the world has to offer, Kiki's outlook on life means that she says "*yes*" far more than she says "*no*", and the stories she can now tell from her escapades around the world make for some excellent dinner party conversation, as well as inspiration for her jewellery collections.

Always one to accept a challenge, and hungry to experience all the world has to offer, Kiki's outook on life means that she says "yes" far more than she says "no"

Kiki in a vintage car on holiday in Cuba

Apollo blue topaz and diamond earrings in 18ct white gold

Apollo tanzantine and diamond pendant

from left to right: Ballerina Lauren Cuthberton, Kiki McDonough,
actress and model Cressida Bonas in the 2019 Special Editions campaign

Cressida Bonas wearing a morganite and diamond collar in the 2019 Special Editions campaign

This model wears detachable earrings and a necklace from the Snowflake collection

2020s

These multi-gemstone stud earrings feature garnets, amethysts, hauyunites, zircons and diamonds set in 18ct yellow gold

THE KIKI TIARA

Though the pandemic did cause much stress and frustration, it also allowed some time to focus on a few shelved ideas, which is how the Kiki Tiara came about. The tiara became popular again in the late 90s, seen decorating the heads of trendy socialites at high-end events. Both a romantic and hierarchical dress code throughout history, the tiara was popularised by the Edwardian elite and royalty and became essential for any married woman wishing to impress at society balls. The rise of high-end jewellery houses such as Cartier and Van Cleef & Arpels saw new designs and an alternate take on a classic piece, and the idea of a tiara as the quintessence of elegance and femininity continued past the early 20th century and well into the modern age.

POSH GIRL: Kiki McDonaugh, the celebrated jewellery designer, is married to Lord Kenilworth. 'This fashion is so pretty and romantic. I think there is a family tiara but I've never seen it. Instead, I have always borrowed different ones.' Platinum and diamonds tiara, c. 1905, by Faberge from Wartski.

"Everybody looks better in a tiara, wearing one changes the way a person walks and holds themselves"

A tiara was required attire for married ladies at the State Opening of Parliament in the 90s, which Kiki attended with Randle, and she opted for a dazzling 1905 Fabergé creation, made from platinum and diamonds. This tiara inspired Kiki to design her own, and this dream finally came to fruition in 2022, the launch coinciding with the platinum jubilee of Queen Elizabeth II. Kiki's design, inspired by a cosmic explosion of stars, is a spectacular work of sparkling brilliant cut diamonds set in 18ct white gold, the shape inspired by the Fabergé tiara she had herself worn some twenty years previous. When worn, the diamond-set details in the tiara's cosmic formation twinkle like the starburst it was designed to reflect. The Kiki Tiara was one of two modern tiaras showcased by the auction house, Sotheby's, as a contemporary example of how tiaras are worn and designed in the modern-day, sitting amongst famous crown jewels and intricate works from famous high jewellery houses. The Kiki Tiara now sits proudly in the Kiki McDonough store in Sloane Square, available for loan and worn by blushing brides.

"After I married Randle, I was lucky enough to go to the Opening of Parliament, where it is custom for married women to wear a tiara. Wartski lent me this Fabergé tiara for the occasion. It was so beautiful and made me feel very special."

16.30ct
Diamonds

18ct
Gold

An illustration of the Kiki Tiara

above: Tally Fosh wearing the Kiki Tiara at her wedding

opposite: The Kiki Tiara features over 1,000 brilliant cut diamonds totalling 16.30ct set in 18ct white gold. Image courtesy of Sotheby's

THE KIKI SUITE

Perhaps the largest social change during Kiki's years in business was the passing of Her Majesty Queen Elizabeth II. A pillar of strength and wisdom during her seventy-year reign, Kiki has noted the late Queen Elizabeth as one of her biggest inspirations, for her steadfastness, dignity, and sense of duty. To commemorate a new era, and the coronation of King Charles III, Kiki designed two dazzling pieces: a diamond sautoir necklace and a pair of diamond earrings. These pieces sat perfectly with the tiara released the previous year and feature intricate diamond work bursting from a central cluster.

The sautoir is a style steeped in royal history. Introduced by French aristocracy in the 18th century, it quickly spread to English nobility where it denoted status, the chain holding precious metals and stones that only the rich could afford. Long and full of movement, this style soon lent itself to the flappers of the Roaring Twenties, with bouncing pendants of fake pearls and cheaper materials, complementary to the defining dress of the era which allowed women to dance and move around freely. Soon after this wave of popularity, the sautoir began decorating the darlings of Hollywood such as Audrey Hepburn and Grace Kelly, cementing it as an iconic jewellery style to stand the test of time. A design that celebrates both old and new, it seemed fitting that a sautoir should mark the introduction of a new King to this modern age.

To accompany the sautoir necklace, Kiki designed a pair of stand-out drop earrings. Large and opulent, the earrings burst with diamonds which catch the light, signifying a nod to the grandeur and excitement of a coronation. Designed to be cherished and passed down the generations (much like the Monarch's crown), the earrings can be worn for celebrations throughout the years.

The Kiki Suite featuring a sautoir necklace and earrings set with brilliant cut diamonds in 18ct white gold

THE CORONATION BROOCH

In addition to designing the *Kiki Suite*, Kiki was approached by Buckingham Palace for a commission of a cypher brooch for Her Majesty Queen Camilla and the Queen's companions, one of which was worn by The Queen's sister, Annabel Elliot, for the coronation of King Charles III on May 6th, 2023. The brooch itself is a stunning piece set with diamonds and crafted in 18ct white gold, in the shape of The Queen's cypher; the letters C and R intertwined, C for Camilla and R for Regina (Latin for 'Queen') with a crown sitting majestically at its point. To thank Kiki for her contribution to the coronation she was presented with a King Charles III Coronation Medal, an esteemed souvenir from His Majesty that Kiki will treasure for life.

top: An illustration of the cypher brooch designed for Her Majesty Queen Camilla and her 'Queen's companions'

above: The Coronation medal awarded to Kiki for her contribution to the King's Coronation

JAZZ

Inspired by Kiki's favourite neoclassical ballet *Elite Syncopations* choreographed by Kenneth McMillan, the *Jazz* collection was designed as a celebration of music and movement. One of Kiki's all-time favourite collections, twenty-three bold cocktail rings were introduced in the summer of 2023, the pieces showcasing vibrant stones such as fire opal, peridot and amethyst. This was also the first time a collection was created using only recycled gold, a decision taken by the brand to reach a more sustainable way of trading. Though Kiki has frequently recycled her gold since she began trading, melting down pieces that didn't sell and using the materials for other collections, this was the first collection to use recycled gold directly from a supplier.

The rings were inspired by the ballet costumes from *Elite Syncopations*, a nod to the unitards with bright, gaudy colours and eye-catching designs, reflective of the highly energetic and dynamic choreography. Kiki wished to emulate the *"powerful riot of colour"* in her designs and, as a result, the rings, much like the playfulness and syncopation in the Ragtime music to which this ballet was set, rejected neat and definitive design and instead embraced eccentricity. A collection which encourages creativity and self-expression, *Jazz* burst onto the Kiki scene and immediately made its mark. This was Kiki's boldest collection yet, with contrasting stones and vivid hues representing her love for playing with colour, and the significant relationship between jewellery design and the ballet was explored from a new, exciting perspective.

"A collection which encourages creativity and self-expression, Jazz burst onto the Kiki scene and immediately made its mark"

This Jazz ring features an octagon step-cut green beryl flanked by two round amethysts and a scattering of diamonds set in 18ct yellow gold

A selection of gemstone rings from the Jazz collection, all set in 18ct yellow gold

*" This collection is like no other that I have ever created in nearly 40 years
in jewellery. I felt so inspired and exhilarated when I looked closely at the
incredible costumes designed by Ian Spurling, in 'Elite Syncopations',
the show that was choreographed so cleverly by Kenneth McMillan.*

*When creating this collection, I pictured those kaleidoscopic scenes that
explode with every colour you could possibly imagine. "*

RUNNING A BUSINESS
IN A PANDEMIC

A decade which began with the trials and tribulations of a global pandemic, the 2020s arrived looking rather bleak. Forced to stay at home and close the store, the future for all businesses seemed, at one point or another, uncertain. For Kiki, a woman whose diary was constantly full to bursting, the lockdown served as both a culture shock and a time for reflection. It was due to a strong online presence that the brand made it through the other end unscathed, and online shopping became its saviour. "*If you wanted to buy a present or treat yourself, you could go to Sainsbury's or Boots*", Kiki says, so people had to trust that they could buy luxury online. With restaurants and bars closed for the foreseeable future and trips abroad impossible, it seemed customers were willing to spend their money elsewhere, indulging in items that would bring them joy. The floor of the store was covered in online orders, and the closing of the high street "*set online shopping forward five years*". When the store opened again, summer arrived with fresh enthusiasm and people were finally allowed to shop in person, the cause of widespread relief, though many people still stayed away. But this reprieve didn't last for long. "*[The UK government] made us lock down four days before Christmas day which was just appalling. Another few days would have made no difference at all, but it would have made a huge difference to retail*". The following four months made Kiki "*speechless with rage*", and she argues that "*the amount of economic and mental health damage [the early 2021] lockdown did was inexcusable*". Press conferences every day with relentless bad news made it feel as if the world was caving in, and the effects of the last lockdown are still being felt by people and businesses across the country. It was an alien and often difficult time for every person during the pandemic, with some of Kiki's team home-schooling and working simultaneously, some not allowed to fly home and see their parents who lived in a different country, some working from their bedrooms in shared flats. Kiki was determined not to furlough anyone in the company long term, so retail staff had to find a way of working without face-to-face contact with customers; virtual consultations, email and online channels, in a completely unfamiliar environment.

Remarkably, the sales of earrings sky-rocketed during the covid year, perhaps due to work Zoom calls and parties meaning people were only half-dressed up, jogging bottoms off camera and party wear on their top halves. A very happy client from Canada emailed the retail team after purchasing a pair of Special Edition morganite earrings to say she wore them every day for home-schooling her children and they had made the whole experience much better. It seemed people were desperate to add a little bit of glamour to an otherwise un-glamorous homebound life. During a period that felt more turbulent and testing than most events in living memory, it was a testament to Kiki's headstrong character, and the perseverance of her entire team, that the brand made it through the other end of the pandemic with little having gone terribly wrong.

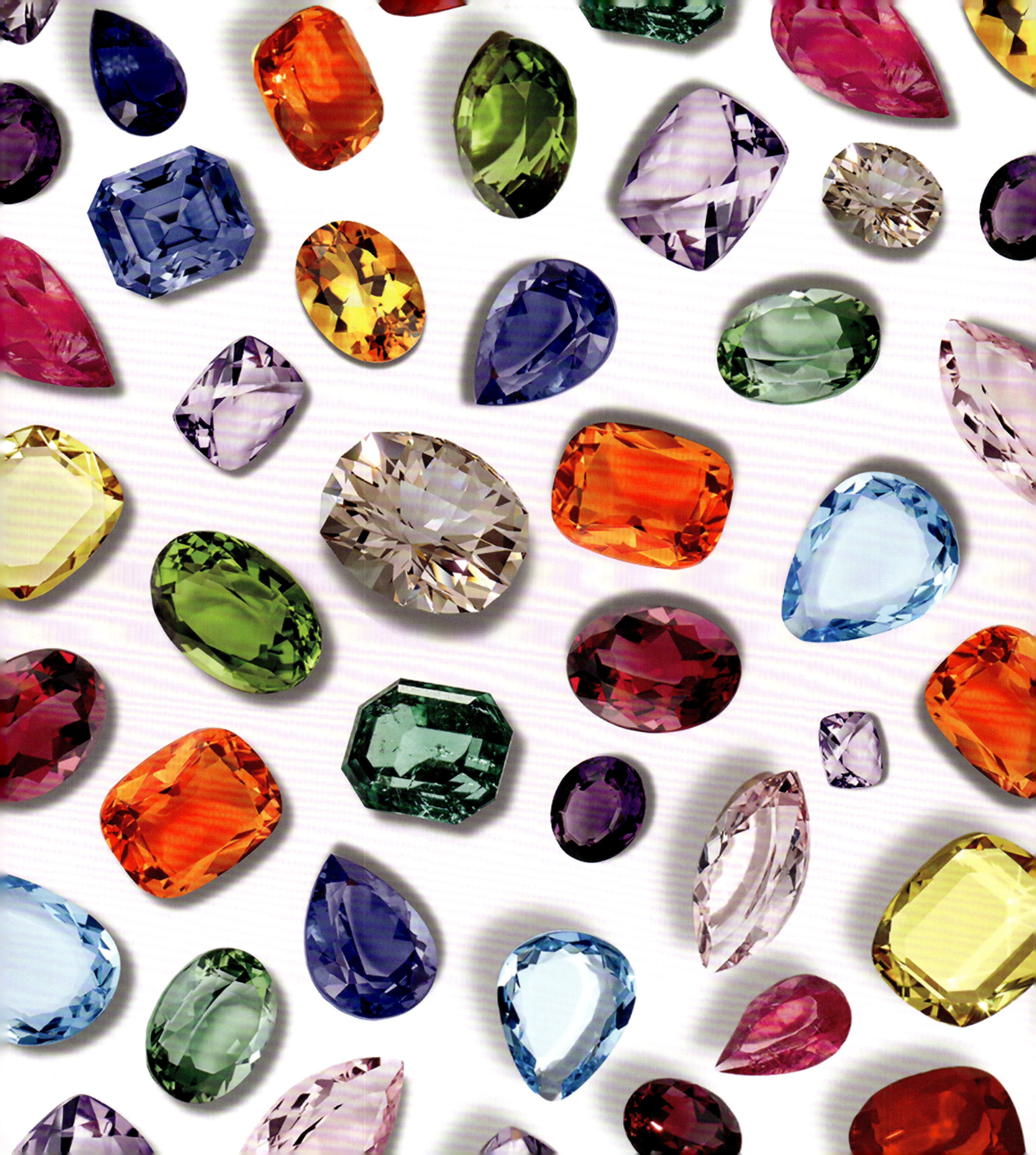

KIKI'S BUSINESS ADVICE

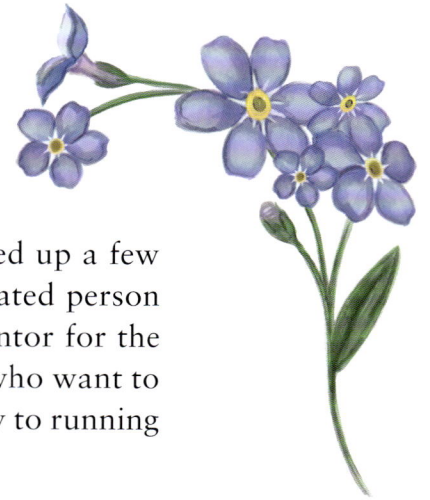

"Forget-Me-Not"

Having been in business for nearly forty years, Kiki has picked up a few tips along the way. A successful business must have a dedicated person at its helm, able to steer it through both highs and lows. As a mentor for the Prince's Trust charity, Kiki often provides advice to young people who want to build their own businesses. According to her, these six things are key to running a successful business:

Luck *How lucky that I did believe that builder who told me Princess Diana was knocking on my door in Elizabeth Street!*

Timing *David having lunch with a friend who had a shop just when I needed one.*

Discipline *It's important in the beginning that you should be first in and last out the door, even if you were up rather late the night before and feel grim! And if you have a store, no answering machine in the middle of the day and no notice on the door saying back in five minutes.*

Charm *Use it whenever you can to get what you want. Charm is a much better way to get what you want than losing your cool.*

"Bubbles"

Discretion *Incredibly important, I learnt this in the first few months of starting this business. I had made a brooch for my friend to give his wife for her birthday, and when I saw his wife at a party a week after he picked it up, I asked her if she was pleased with her present. Her birthday wasn't for another week, and I had accidentally ruined the surprise. From that day to this, I have never once asked a client about their jewellery unless they bring it up first.*

Talent *This is obviously very important but without everything else, your talent won't survive.*

"Candy"

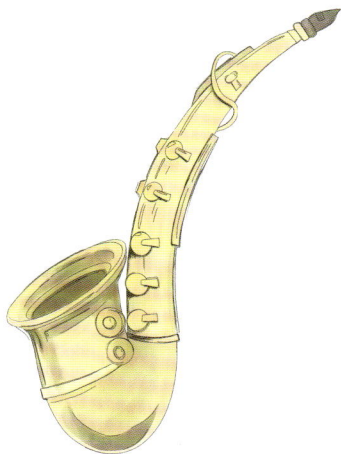

"Jazz"

"Lauren"

"Carousel"

Starting and maintaining a growing business takes a lot of hard work, and Kiki has built up her team over the years, learning how to delegate and transition in an ever-changing economic and technological landscape. Her first hire was a PA for three days a week in the late 80s, and the introduction of her mother to the shop floor in Elizabeth Street helped to ease the load for another few years. She did have a board of directors early on, but, given certain disagreements, it wasn't to last long, so she decided to build the brand using only her own initiative. It wasn't until she moved to her flagship store on Symons Street that the business really grew, going from five employees to over twenty. As always, slow and steady wins the race, and Kiki advocates for a slow-paced and careful start. *"If you do it a bit slower, you build a much more solid base. I think that those who run before they can walk are making a mistake"*. It may not feel natural, and sometimes Kiki wants to go slightly quicker than the brand is ready for. She credits her Managing Director, Sian Daley, for her considered approach to the company, wanting to take it forward in the right direction rather than simply taking it forward. And, whilst business is important, it is not more important than other parts of life, and a strong foundation means that the other things, family and friends, can come first too.

The team has expanded in ways that Kiki couldn't have foreseen forty years ago. The company now has structure and departments across operations, production, merchandising, wholesale, visual merchandising and multiple departments within PR+ marketing and digital commerce. Kiki McDonough has evolved into a recognisable brand with a strong DNA of colour, craftsmanship, and quality. As the decades fly by, one important pillar of focus has been on sustainability and supply chain transparency. Joining the Responsible Jewellery Council (RJC) in 2021, the world's leading sustainability standard-setting organisation for the jewellery and watch industry, was a necessary step for the brand. Most of the brand's supply chain was also in the process of receiving their own RJC accreditation or similar, ensuring all sourced gemstones were conflict-free and every worker treated fairly, and all parties were keen to find a way of working together responsibly. Work continues in this area and is embedded in the company's strategy, with initiatives such as planting a tree for every purchase on the Kiki McDonough website implemented as a way of offsetting carbon usage, an attempt to ensure a positive future and a healthy planet for the next generation. Consumers are now more aware of sustainability, and the impact materials and production can have on our environment. They want to shop consciously, with faith in an ethical supply chain, and every business has a duty to make sustainability a top priority. Purchasing fine jewellery will always be a considered choice, and the beauty of the fine jewellery industry and the hardwearing, precious materials used within it allow pieces to be passed down through the generations, so it is not subject to waste and overconsumption issues. Fine jewellery should be treasured, and Kiki McDonough wants the pieces it sells to be worthy of that special treatment.

A TRIP TO
THE FUNFAIR

As a child, Kiki's father would take her to the funfair at Battersea Park once a year as a treat, where she would ride the carousel and brave the waterslide. Kiki's love of rides and theme parks has continued throughout her life. She remembers going to Thorpe Park with her boys when they were small, rolling her eyes at their distaste for her favourite rides and making them wait for her as she rode the rapids three times. The idea of a funfair has always invoked memories of simple fun and childlike innocence, and, even now, visiting the funfair or an amusement park brings out Kiki's inner child. In honour of this, the *Carousel* collection was launched with circular motifs in vibrant, glinting colours to represent the dizzying motion of a carousel ride. Spotlighting an array of gemstones including multi-coloured sapphires, aquamarines, beryls, tanzanites, and tourmalines, the baguette shape of these stones was inspired by the panelling on carousel ceilings. Also in this collection are four pairs of statement curl earrings with freeform sapphires, each one unique in shape, which remind Kiki of the decorated horses on carousel rides, each with their individual names, colours, and striking patterns. This collection encourages everyone to reminisce, and is a nostalgic nod to the innocent joy of being swept around in circles on the back of a bobbing horse.

" The idea of a funfair has always
invoked memories of simple fun
and childlike innocence "

Two pairs of earrings from the Carousel collection, featuring baguette gemstones in 18ct yellow gold

Maria Cecília Frering in the orange and green sapphire curl earrings from the Carousel collection

Maria Cecília Frering and Riyaq Hassan in Kiki Classics blue topaz and peridot stud earrings,
released in 2024, and a Grace blue topaz ring

FIREWORKS

A vibrant spectacle of sparks and colour bursting in breathtaking shapes and patterns, fireworks have lit up special occasions for decades, and what better way to commemorate an important anniversary than with a collection inspired by the act of celebration? Featuring a kaleidoscope of colourful gemstones, this new collection was the perfect way to mark forty dazzling years of Kiki McDonough and was the brand's most colourful launch yet. Like a brilliant fireworks display, the pieces in this collection were designed to draw attention, make an impact, and inject an electrifying burst of colour.

Fireworks earrings featuring amethyst, peridot, fire opal, blue topaz, citrine, and diamonds

top left: Fireworks earrings featuring amethyst,
blue topaz, and peridot with diamond accents

top right: Fireworks earrings featuring fire opal,
lavender amethyst, citrine, and diamonds

right: Fireworks ring featuring blue topaz, fire opal,
lavender amethyst, citrine, peridot, and diamonds

THE BIG FOUR

To celebrate four decades of business, the four Kiki necklaces were designed to spotlight Kiki's four favourite gemstones: fire opal, morganite, peridot, and blue topaz. Inspired by the ballet *Jewels* by George Balanchine in which each movement portrays a precious gem and its history, the ballet is set to specially selected music from the composers Fauré, Stravinsky, and Tchaikovsky to portray three locations in specific periods. Emeralds spotlight elegant France in the late 1800s, the fiery roaring 20s in New York for Rubies, and the grandeur and opulence of Imperial Russia are celebrated in the third act; 'Diamonds'. Like *Jewels*, Kiki's *Big Four* showcases gemstones that have played an integral part in the history of Kiki McDonough, with each stone symbolising an important part of Kiki's journey. Fire opal represents the pioneering introduction of exciting and lesser-known gemstones to the business, morganite signifies Kiki's love for ballet and the impact it has had on her designs, peridot's summer green has long been Kiki's favourite, and versatile blue topaz has been claimed by Kiki's customers as their most-loved gemstone of all time. After months of sourcing the perfect gemstones, these necklaces were designed to show off each gem and their distinctive characters, whilst memorialising each 'movement' of the brand in glorious technicolour.

Oval and round peridot gemstones are interspersed with diamond petal detailing in this striking necklace

*This necklace features orange and red fire opals in oval, round,
and pear cuts, with sparkling diamond accents throughout*

above: An illustration of 'The Big Four' blue topaz necklace

opposite: An elegant diamond bow cascades through oval and round blue topaz gemstones in this blue topaz collar necklace worn by Lauren Cuthbertson

*Dazzling diamond daisy motifs complement beautiful ballet-pink morganites
in oval, pear, and cushion cuts in this necklace*

An illustration of 'The Big Four' morganite necklace

WHAT THE FUTURE HOLDS

Looking back on forty years, it is easy to feel as if time has simply disappeared, and it is important to pause and reflect. "*I don't think I've changed*", Kiki muses, "*even after all the things that have happened to me, and all the times that I've lived through*". She is now able to sit back and look at what she has created, and is lovingly surrounded by people who have been with her through it all: her two sons, her two supportive ex-husbands who remain good friends, her partner Matthew, the people who have worked for her including her Managing Director, Sian Daley, and the countless friends she has made along the way. Kiki has maintained a great relationship with many of her employees, and at the thirtieth-anniversary dinner for the brand in 2015, every PA who had ever worked for her was in attendance. Building a brand that is loved and championed by women of multiple generations is a victory, and there is something to be learned from the way Kiki has managed to stand the mighty test of time.

Success is difficult to define and constantly changing. For Kiki, in the beginning, success was moving to her first stand-alone store, making it through a recession, seeing one of her pieces in Vogue. It is now watching her designs be worn by Her Majesty The Queen and HRH The Princess of Wales, expanding her customer base worldwide, a flagship store in Sloane Square, at the heart of one of London's key shopping districts. Success is her family, raising her two sons into well-rounded, kind men. It is looking back and feeling proud of what she has achieved, both professionally and personally. For Kiki, building the brand has been an "*extraordinary journey full of everything [she] could have ever wished for*", and the future is bright. The brand is expanding and ever-changing, and Kiki will be there for as long as she is able to stand. "*I will never reach contentment because I don't have that character*", she says. There are always more people to meet, more events to attend, more gemstones to collect. She will most likely follow in her mother's footsteps, still turning up to the office at ninety years old, sharp as a tack. Over forty years Kiki has designed countless collections, introduced several coloured gemstones to the jewellery market, and injected colour and joy into everything her company has produced. Her flagship store remains a place people are keen to visit, friendly and welcoming, and her jewellery will be worn and cherished for years to come. There is still so much Kiki wants to achieve, and she will face this the way she has always faced business: carefully, smartly, and with a great sense of humour, so that her team is inspired to continue the journey with her.

Three rings from the 2025 Everyday Gold collection featuring citrine, fire opal, blue topaz, peridot, and lavender amethyst gemstones set in 18ct yellow gold

CREDITS

Kiki would like to thank the following for their contribution to this book:

Illustrations throughout the book by: Harriet Gracie, Maria Cecília Frering, Samantha Fleur Camp.

Photographs: Frontis, 150, 154-155: © Adshot, Gianluca De Girolamo; 6, 10, 15, 27, 34, 35, 40, 45, 50, 51, 56, 61, 62, 65, 66, 67, 68, 71, 72 bottom, 74, 75 left, 76, 77, 78, 79, 80, 81, 83, 84, 86, 87, 88, 89, 91, 97, 98, 99, 102, 105, 108, 109, 110, 111, 114 bottom, 123, 124, 125, 126, 127, 129, 132, 136, 140, 141, 145, 147, 164, 165, 166, 168, 172: © Judita Kunisktye; 12, 47, 63, 75 right, 95, 96, 117, 121, 151, 162, 163, 167, 169: © Ollo Weguelin; 26, 28, 33, 37, 46, 85, 100, 104, 106, 161, 175: © Hanover Saffron Ltd, Philip Crinnan; 64, 128, 142, 143: © Elizabeth Gibson; 42 bottom: © Georgina Viney; 43: © Antoinette Eugster; 48, 133: © Getty Images; 53: Social Stereotypes: words by Victoria Mather, illustration by Sue Macartney-Snape; 59, 72 top, 82, 144, 152: Art Director: Chris Lowe, Stylist: Milena Mihic, Hair & Makeup: Ruth Warrior; photographs © Ray Brown Agency, Christopher Fenner; 90: © Adam Fussell, courtesy of Luxury London magazine; 107: top © Chris Howlett; 116: © Jem Mitchell; 131: © Carla Guler, Art Director/ Fashion Stylist: Nicole Smallwood, Model: Gia Tan, courtesy of Country & Town House magazine; 135, 148: © Tom Durn; 134 right: © Phil Yorkshire; 134 left: © Kate Bulford; 137: © Zoe Griffin; 149: © Sotheby's; 170: © Willie Christie.

We gratefully acknowledge the permission granted to use these images. Every possible attempt has been made to identify and contact copyright holders. Any errors or omissions are inadvertent and will be corrected in subsequent editions.

I would like to thank my publisher Alexandra Papadakis, for the creation of this beautiful book, Aldo Sampieri for his elegant design, and Molly Dewar for her editorial and production work.